OVERCOMING DELAY FACTORS IN DELIVERANCE

Patrick I. Odigie

OVERCOMING DELAY FACTORS IN DELIVERANCE
Copyright © 2017 by Patrick I. Odigie

ISBN: 978-0-9987923-2-3

Published by: Prophetic Power House Inc. New York
Editing
Praise Odigie
Lara Olutumbi
Pastor Gbenga Showumi
Ola Aboderin
Rosanda Richardson

Cover design by Bodunrin Akinyanju and Divine Mathew
For more copies of this book and all our messages and training materials please contact:
Patrick I. Odigie
Post Office Box 830, Uniondale NY 11553
516 499-2350
Email: propheticpowerhouse@yahoo.com
Website: www.patrickodigie.com

TABLE OF
CONTENTS

Dedication

To the one Eternal God, the Creator of all things, both visible and invisible.

To the Lord Jesus who loves me completely. Going all the way, He drank the full cup of the wrath of the Almighty God in my stead.

To the Blessed Eternal Spirit of Grace, my Counselor, Teacher, and Ever-Patient Coach be all the glory always, now and forever! I love you till eternity my God.

Acknowledgement

In Africa, we say, "it takes a village to raise a child." To stay on the true path of life and attempting to share some beneficial truths through these series is made possible by three generations of generous human beings whose love, sacrifice and faith in me have greatly enriched my life's journey and purpose. I hereby register my deepest appreciation to a long list of spiritual Fathers and Mothers, faithful friends and spiritual children too numerous to list here.

Standing strong with me in love and mustering every ounce of energy to keep me moving is my precious wife, Pastor Mabel Odigie and of course, on our side, are three very loving and understanding children: Praise, Honor, and Favor all cheering us and bearing long with us in this tough undertaking called life. You are my earthly treasure, and I can't wait to share your noisy neighborhood in Heaven.

Finally, to my powerful editing team for these series, my most profound thanks. Ms. Nadine Thomas who did initial transcribing; my daughters Omolara Olutunbi and Praise Odigie for great editing work on this book. Further professional editing was done by Pastor Gbenga Showumi, Ola Aboderin, and Rosanda Richardson. You have all labored so hard. Thank you. The author accepts responsibility for any observable errors and welcomes your feedback.

For many believers in Christ, addressing the myriad of internal conflicts, endless struggles, and contradictions that daily confront them definitely require spiritual grit and determination. There is also need to lift spiritual curtains and expose the secret layers of hidden demonic contaminations tucked away in a remote past of generational demonic influences and corruptions.

Hidden demonic covenants, curses, and a laundry list of self-inflicted wounds resulting from inappropriate interactions with controlling territorial demonic powers through ignorance and carelessness must be uncovered and cleared out. The ability to break free and live a meaningful, productive, and fulfilling life calls for addressing critical issues in deliverance and aggressive warfare.

Unfortunately, large sections of the Body of Christ are burdened with little understanding of effective deliverance training, and the devil's business thrives on ignorance. This needless darkness has proven to be problematic, leaving many genuine believers stuck at the crossroads of unidentified conflicts, delays, painful losses, and frustrations.

The Word of God declares, *"My people are destroyed for lack of knowledge"* (Hosea 4:6). The Holy Spirit, writing through the Apostle Paul, admonishes us to be abreast of Satan's devices: *"Lest Satan should get an advantage of us: for we are not ignorant of his devices"* (2 Corinthians 2:11).

There is indeed much to thank God for in Deliverance Ministry today. However, much of the practice of deliverance ministry in this generation on closer observation seems deficient of a real sound scriptural foundation. Just the other day, I heard a well-meaning and respectable deliverance minister define Deliverance as the act of casting out devils. This individual is a true laborer in the Kingdom but his incomplete understanding of the operational definition of deliverance, like many other well-meaning servants of God, engenders serious problems as it sets out on a faulty premise.

If we embark on a journey without knowing where we are headed, how can we know for sure that we ultimately have reached our destination? While the process of deliverance entails casting out of demons, it is far more than that; you cannot cast out sin, and while we are commanded to mortify the flesh, we can neither cast out the flesh nor the world we live in and these all impact on our deliverance from day to day.

The preaching of deliverance is prevalent, and the true teaching of deliverance is scarce and much limited in scope. What is the implication of this? While preaching can warn and motivate a desire for a change of outcomes, it is sound teaching in all wisdom that can impart the actual 'know-how' to secure those desirable outcomes.

This is why every believer must be armed with the adequate knowledge of the principles, purposes, and processes of total deliverance from the works of the devil. What Christ purchased for us with His Blood is total freedom from everything that is contrary to God's desire for our lives. Until this is achieved, no true believer must relent.

It is in furtherance of this goal of absolute freedom in Christ that this three-volume book has been written. The first volume – Foundations for True and Complete Deliverance – dwelt on the meaning, necessity, and ramifications of deliverance. In this volume, Overcoming Delay Factors in Deliverance, I aim to address critical questions on this important subject. I expect that this book will be used by deliverance workers, spiritual warfare workers, and ministers of the Gospel to help them really understand the subject in depth.

It is my prayer that as you read, you will experience Holy Spirit-inspired enlightenment that will position you for total emancipation from every bondage and limitation.

Foreword

Rev. Patrick has been a friend for many years. It was an honor to be asked to write the foreword for this book: Overcoming Delay Factors in Deliverance. In my friendship with Patrick over the years, I can attest to his fervent love for The Lord and his great desire to see the people of God free wherever he is opportune to minister. This book is the natural fruit of the Calling of God in his life. The knowledge he has gained and the lessons he has learned through his faithful walk with God are now at your fingertips.

Over the years, the issue of deliverance has been a hot topic in the church. Unfortunately, many in the church have no clue what to make of it. There is no doubt that deliverance has been misused for petty reasons. However, a genuine Biblical Christian will definitely believe that deliverance is part of the redemption story.

I firmly believe that it is the will of God for all His children to be free from every stronghold of the devil.

This Bible speaks eloquently that the Lord God Almighty desires all His children to live free from the corruption of the flesh and spirit.

"Therefore, having these promises, beloved, let us cleanse ourselves from all defilement of flesh and spirit, perfecting holiness in the fear of God." (2 Corinthians 7:1 NASB)

I also believe that holiness in the Christian's life will be definitely interrupted if the defilement inside him or her is not dealt with. It is not just enough to be saved from the life of sin, but we must enjoy all the benefits of the Cross. The Blood of Jesus is what does the cleansing of our flesh and spirit.

I greatly encourage all Christians everywhere to avail themselves of this masterfully written book: Overcoming Delay Factors in Deliverance. It is an eye opener to truly live a worthy Christian life before God and men. The author has done a very extensive work under the leading of the Holy Spirit. Writing this book as a Prophet/Teacher of the Word, you can rest assured that the Good Hand of God is upon him. His personal life testifies to the truth revealed in this book. You are encouraged to recommend it to everyone in your sphere of influence. The content of this book is biblically sound and the Lord Himself will not leave you without blessing your life now and always. May the Lord have His way in all of our lives. Amen.

Pastor Michael C Mordi
Senior Pastor
Wind and Fire International Christian Center
Rochester Minesota United States of America

Three Sources of Demonic Trouble

How do demons gain access into people's lives to cause trouble and inflict harm? What loopholes do they exploit? There are vast amount of literature; therefore my emphasis will be on the major areas of concern.

1. The Congregation of the Dead

"The man that wandereth out of the way of understanding shall remain in the congregation of the dead." (Proverbs 21:16).

Membership of what the Bible calls the "congregation of the dead" is an automatic ticket for demonic infiltration, infestation, manifestation, and oppression. The Amplified Bible renders the above verse thus: "a man who wanders out of the way of understanding shall abide in the congregation of the spirits of the dead" while The Message Bible says "**Whosoever wanders off the straight and narrow ends up in the congregation of ghosts.**" In other words, if you are not planted in Christ Jesus and growing in His knowledge and grace, then you will automatically remain in the congregation of the dead.

To understand what I mean by the congregation of the dead, you need to understand what the congregation of life is. The head of the congregation of life is the Living God. Any member of the congregation of life has his or her name maintained in the record of the Lamb's Book of Life. This is after you have given your life to Christ.

To put it simply, any man or woman born into this world is dead on arrival. "Dead," here, means spiritually disconnected from the Living God, and as the Bible puts it, "**cut off from the commonwealth of Israel**" (Ephesians 2:12); that is, not enlisted in God's covenant or inheritance.

Every man arrives on earth dead spiritually. Any person who is not in Christ remains among the congregation of the dead with their names in the Book of the Dead. The head of the dead is Lucifer.

So, how does the congregation of the dead function? First, there is membership. As I said, Lucifer is the head; and for membership, he has the principalities and powers, the rulers of darkness, and the hosts of spiritual wickedness in high places, plus men and women, who consciously enlist in and serve the purpose of the devil. They all constitute the congregation of the dead.

The congregation of the dead is territorially cut off from the life of God. The Almighty God is at once Light, Love, and Life (Eternal life or Zoe).   He that has the Son has life (1 John 5:12). Since the Fall of Lucifer and the subsequent Fall of Man, territories in the vast known and unknown parts of the universe, besides the third heaven - the Throne of God - have been invaded by Lucifer and his demons.

There are satanic princes, the rulers of darkness, who are behind the secret things of this world and are in charge of the

"Membership of what the Bible calls the "congregation of the dead" is an automatic ticket for demonic infiltration, infestation, manifestation, and oppression... if you are not planted in Christ Jesus and growing in His knowledge and grace, then you will automatically remain in the congregation of the dead."

different nations. Adam sold out his lease on the earth to the devil. For that matter, every nation has a ruler, a demonic prince, which controls its affairs. Every state, city, community or family has a spiritual ruler.

A typical nuclear family, for instance, consists of father, mother, and the children; but that is not all. There is also a spiritual component. The father and the mother have the spiritual authority over the family structure and, of course, the spiritual dimension is controlled by the demon spirits or fallen angels, if such a family is not in a covenant relationship with the Almighty God.

Usually, in most traditional societies, cosmological orientation presupposes an existing symbiotic relationship between the spiritual and the physical. In the physical, people see themselves as representatives and extensions of their ancestors who are still somewhere in the spiritual realm and actively participating in the everyday life of the family or community. Their ancestors who died and passed on are regarded as having transited to a higher plain of life (spirit realm) but are still seen as valid members of the family. For this reason, in most traditional societies, various sacrifices, libations, and oblations are done as an act of worship or appeasement by representatives of those who have passed on to the spirit realm to enlist the help of the dead.

However, the Bible says it is appointed unto a man once to die and after that the judgment (Hebrews 9:27). In other words, earthly life ends the state of man's control over his family. Once you are dead, you face judgment. If your life was not lived in Christ Jesus, you are heading straight to hell.

There is no such thing as some ancestors being able to intercede for the living. The concept of engaging the help of forefathers or the worship of dead saints or ancestors is Satan's ploy to infiltrate the destiny of the misinformed, thereby perpetuating himself in the generations of a family, holding them in captivity, and transferring destruction from one generation to another.

Typically, therefore, when we offer worship to our forefathers, there is a demonic prince in the family acting as the ancestral spirit, receiving worship, limiting that family, and implementing the prescribed destruction of Lucifer. But it doesn't end there. Every child coming into that family is assigned a demon spirit, and that demon spirit is a familiar of such a child in the spiritual realm. It is an angel of Satan delegated to monitor and mold the life of that child according to the program of Lucifer. That is why the Bible says, you and I were dead in trespasses and sins when we were in the womb or the grave of sin.

Here is the exact quote: "**And you hath he quickened, who were dead in trespasses and sins; Wherein in time past ye walked according to the course of this world, according to the prince of the power of the air, the spirit that now worketh in the children of disobedience: Among whom also we all had our conversation in times past in the lusts of our flesh, fulfilling the desires of the flesh and of the mind; and were by nature the children of wrath, even as others**" (Ephesians 2:1-3).

It declares, right from the beginning, that we used to be among the congregation of the dead. We have, however, been quickened. 'Quickened' means being raised to life and having been forgiven of all our sins and trespasses. It goes further to say that when we were in the grave, we conducted our lives according to the dictates of the program of the prince of the power of the air, which is the devil, among whom we once had our lifestyles the same spirit that controls the children of disobedience to this day.

Typically, the spiritual dimension of an unsaved family is coordinated by Satan's representative of that family, the ancestral spirit, who delegates demons to the family members. At times, some people might see their fathers or mothers or relatives in their dreams, but it may just be demonic manipulation. It may simply be the demonic familiars of such relatives masquerading in the dreams to confuse and depress those who are not spiritually informed about such matters. If you are saved and believe in dreams, you still need to exercise discernment to avoid demonic manipulations.

This can be a real source of trouble for some people undergoing deliverance, especially if they are individuals from families where there were types of inherent occult abilities. There is a level of common cross-border bondage that, even if one of the family members becomes born-again, Satan would want to start to channel the flow of evil from other members of the family.

Simply put, when you give your life to Christ, the devil immediately regards you as a rebel against the family authority. That is why, for a born-again person, while it is necessary that you honor your father and your mother, you must be answerable to only God's Holy Spirit. If your parents continue to control your life, then that spiritual authority that works in them will hold sway in your life.

This is often the biggest area of trouble for many because when you are looking at major sources of demonic trouble, the biggest of it all is through

> *"...when you give your life to Christ, the devil immediately regards you as a rebel against the family authority"*

the door of inheritance. Inherited curses and generational curses derive from the generations of struggle, pain, and demonic involvement of the family which continues to hold sway. By the Law of God, the things that a father does could have influence or effect for at least four generations. If your fathers, up to 400 years ago, were worshippers of idols, were involved in the occult, or were involved in witchcraft, those things still have spiritual relevance in your very life until you address them. You can do that through personal deliverance and aggressive, sustained, ongoing warfare to disconnect yourself from the flow of evil; and also to help other members of your family to be free from the evil effect of such satanic covenants.

One of the biggest issues in deliverance is generational curses. The delegated family spirit maintains a file on the life of individuals in the family and trains each child according to the program of the devil. Naturally, most people will not acknowledge this. They prefer to think that they are living their own lives, but the life they are living outside of Christ is a dictate of the devil.

The Apostle Paul, by the Holy Spirit, made some crucial observations in 1 Corinthians 12 concerning spiritual gifts. However, when you consider the lifestyle of the Corinthian church, you find an anomaly. Despite being so blessed with spiritual gifts, they had embarrassingly low morals - getting drunk during Communion (1 Corinthians 11:20-21) and having a man boasting of sleeping with his father's wife (1 Corinthians 5). Thus, as Paul began to intercede for them, God revealed some things to him, which led to his remarks in the twelfth chapter:

"...brethren, I would not have you ignorant. Ye know that ye were Gentiles, carried away unto these dumb idols, even as ye were led." In other words, there were certain things that characterized the lives of the Corinthians, which were not of their own making. They had been hijacked from the path of destiny that God had prepared for them. Sad to say, the destinies of many great lives, families, churches and whole nations are often hijacked by vicious spiritual powers and hardly anyone is speaking of it. God's servants, please raise up a war cry!

God said something to Jeremiah in Jeremiah 1:5, which could also be applied to every other person on earth. **"Before I formed thee in the belly I knew thee, and before thou camest forth out of the womb I sanctified thee, and I ordained thee a prophet unto the nations."** Yes, God has a program; He had a purpose for you before you were conceived but this can also be affected by the roots of your family. This is where Christians who have had two or three generations of ministers in their family line before they arrived will have things a little easier. And by the way, even if your father and mother are born-again, every battle they did not succeed in fighting will be passed on to you.

The Christian life is a serious business; IT IS WAR! The moment you give your life to Christ, you have declared war. Once you are born-again, you are disconnected and removed from the congregation of the dead, and the devil fights you desperately.

Something very interesting is recorded in John 11:38-44. Jesus had come to the tomb of Lazarus, His friend, who had been dead and He (Jesus) was to raise him from the dead. People, including the sisters of Lazarus, did not believe that this could happen. Anyway, Jesus went to the tomb and raised Lazarus from the dead.

The Bible has some striking observations about that encounter. As Jesus prayed a simple prayer, calling Lazarus out of the grave, we notice that Lazarus came out in response to Jesus, but there were certain conditions that continued to persist that needed to be dealt with. **"And he that was dead came forth, bound hand and foot with graveclothes: and his face was bound about with a napkin. Jesus saith unto them, 'Loose him, and let him go'"** (v. 44).

Please take note. Jesus had called Lazarus out of the grave. But there were some grave conditions, which still identified him as a member of the congregation of the dead, although he had been brought out of it. He had life; he was not dead anymore. However, the Bible says that when he came forth, he was still bound hand and feet. If you are bound in your hand, you cannot accomplish goals. If you are bound at your feet, your movement (meaning progress) is restrained. Grave clothes are a personal identification with the grave; which means demons will follow you as long as you have on those clothes.

Moreover, Lazarus' face was bound about, which means that he couldn't see. He had no vision. These are very serious realities in the life of people, and, as I said, it is most often one's family of origin and the things they had indulged in that will present the greatest source of trouble. If the father of the family, even to the third or fourth generation, was an occult member, everybody in that family line is enlisted spiritually in that occult system. That is why some people may never directly participate in some occult things, but they will have occult experiences. They will have difficulties getting ahead in life because of occult bondages.

Jesus said that those of a man's household shall be his worst enemies (Matthew 10:36), which means that your greatest source of trouble is not the person you meet on the job or the difficulties you think you have - it is often from your roots. That is where your greatest battles and warfare will originate. It is not the only source but the greatest and the fiercest. WHY? Because you were a member of a certain structure called the congregation of the dead. While you were there, you were a common inheritor of satanic debts and liabilities, and demons who are part of that covenant will want to collect from you throughout your entire life until you apply the Blood, break the curse, and stand up in warfare on your behalf and behalf of your other family members.

Understanding the demonic bondage, occult bondage, ancestral spirits, and common inherited curses on the family line will help you to take decisive steps in seeking deliverance to get yourself loose and to get your family members loose, including your children. As I earlier noted, this trend has a generational side. The enemy wants to perpetuate the constraints, pains, and oppression from generation to generation. You, the born-again Spirit-filled believer, are the curse-breaker of the family!

2.   Territorial Demonic Pollutions

Another source of demonic trouble is what I will call territorial bondage, territorial exposure or territorial infestation. How does territorial bondage occur? I mentioned before that there are ruling powers in various territories. These ruling powers are behind the scenes, orchestrating conditions in communities. Certain communities behave in a certain way; certain nations dwell upon certain things that make them anti-God and anti-Christ. Certain cultures and popular trends are mere manifestations of the identity of the ruling principality in that locality.

So, if you are born in a particular locality, most of the things you are participating in are generated and controlled by that ruling principality, and they will have inroads into your life. If you attend a school in a particular locality, most of the things that are going on socially or culturally are demonically controlled from behind the scene. So when you just look at the attractions and seeming benefits, and you jump on board, what you do not know is that you are opening your destiny to the control of those demons.

The point here is that certain things become part of your life just by you being born, raised or educated in a particular territory. And even if you are born-again but do not know how to consecrate yourself, these forces will bring you under what I call containment by introducing some of their popular cultures to your life. This is why born-again Christians have to be people who can be discerning and decisive on what they permit into their lives. We are responsible to God for what we permit in our lives.

Territorial pollutions could also come through participation in religious activities that are anti-Gospel. Mind you, some of such activities occur even in churches! There are churches with serious occult foundations. If one of these is your family church and you are a part of it, doing all the things they do in that kind of setting, you are going to have a fight. If you do not know, the much you do not know will make you much more vulnerable and exploitable.

I will give you a personal example. I was born into idolatry, and as I grew up, for survival purposes, my mother enlisted in a church which we thought was a remarkable one because the people had the ability to see visions and revelations. The prophets could tell you almost anything about your life. What we did not realize at that time was that those seemingly prophetic abilities were not from the Holy Spirit but were manifestations of occult abilities.

Because I used to be a member of such a church, I feel free in my heart to mention it specifically in the event any person is reading this, they will be better informed ahead. I was a member of the Celestial Church of Christ for eight years before I met and gave my life to Christ. The Celestial Church of Christ is not a proper Gospel church; it is an occult-based church. There are many such occult-based churches. They are syncretic, having a pretentious appearance of serving God. Many members are innocent and, I should say, deceived so that they may fall into the category of deceived deceivers.

When I was a member of this church, we (the so-called prophets and I) frequently fought over the women. Sometimes a prophet and I would be dating the same woman. One of the distinguishing heritages of occult-based churches and prophets is promiscuity. People truly seeking God may go to such churches, but they will end up opening their lives to more demons just by being in the environment and participating in the activities.

> *"... born-again Christians really have to be people who are discerning and decisive on what they permit into their lives."*

If you have been a member one of these churches, when, by the mercy of God, you later come to the knowledge of Christ, you will have some battles because those forces will try to take advantage of you and sneak into your new experience to destroy you. You have to discern what they are properly, neutralize the Covenants, and you have to be taken through deliverance and then grow in the knowledge of the Scriptures.

I must also mention here that a few years ago, God gave me seven points for Pentecostal churches. He said if Pentecostal churches do not pay attention to these seven points, they will become semi-occult churches. I am amazed at how many Pentecostal churches have been invaded by occult practices. Some of them pretend to be prophetic churches, but they are not. You can read about those seven points towards the end of this book. But the point I was making is that your territory includes where you were born, where you grew up, where you were educated, and whether you were involved in any religion other than authentic Bible Christianity. All of these will open you up, just by being in that environment.

3. Personal Involvement or Flirtation with the Devil

A third source of demonic trouble is personal involvement in things that are demonically controlled. For instance, we join certain pseudo-social clubs which appear to have humanitarian orientations but are rooted in occultism. Participation in such activities as New Age directly opens people up to demonic infestation. Visiting false prophets or occult people, such as palm readers, is a doorway to demonic influences in the life of an individual. Tarot card reading and séances will also open the doorway to the occult realm. Believing in or reading horoscopes will open the doorway. These are things that people do on their own that create problems for them.

Moreover, there are types of music and works of art that are inspired from the demonic realm for the purpose of binding the souls of men. Many of the popular artists you see today have a covenant with the devil, and their record labels and releases have curses on them. When you dwell on them, then you open yourself up. These are self-inflicted demonic conditions. When you begin to expose yourself to cartoons and pictures that are vile and corrupt or those with occult undertones, they constitute a doorway that could open you up to demonic pollution and manifestation.

One of the biggest doors also is a sexual violation, and for that purpose, the enemy always pushes it. In fact, for many young people, from the age of five to seven, the enemy will make every effort to access them sexually, and when they are so violated, he puts demons of immorality and rebellion in them. When they get to their teenage years, those things will show up.

Any sexual relationship outside of marriage is an open doorway to demonic infestation, pollution, and ultimately, oppression. There are some that are very serious in nature. There are some people male and female - who are agents of Satan, and

> *"Any sexual relationship outside of marriage is an open doorway to demonic infestation, pollution, and ultimately, oppression.*

they go about pushing for sex. When you engage in sex with such people, your destiny is taken, and you are no longer the same. Many people get into trouble this way without realizing it.

There are some very terrible cases I have seen in this regard. There was a young girl of twelve years who lived with her sister. The sister's boyfriend came one day, took the girl away to the Bush, violated her, and wiped her off. In adulthood, she found out that her menses did not flow. This was treated medically, but it was not a medical condition; it was demonic.

There are many cases of people who are seeking occult powers for money-making, and they look for young girls or young men to sleep with, and after that collect their body fluids for money-making rituals. Someone may enter into a sexual relationship willingly or unwillingly, and when they get out of it, their destiny may become totally destroyed. It takes the grace and the mercy of God to recover from these conditions; but with God, all things are possible.

BREAKTHROUGH PROPHETIC DELIVERANCE PRAYERS

1. I repent and receive your forgiveness for wandering away from instruction and refusing wise counsel. Lord restore all my vandalized virtues due to past ignorance and stubbornness.

2. Every doorway into the congregation of the dead, I shut you now in the mighty name of Jesus. Every influence of dead and the grave in my life and destiny be liquidated now in the name of Jesus.

3. Every covenant with untimely death, Death of aspirations, opportunities, dreams and visions, be revoked and nullified now in Jesus' name.

4. Let the Blood of Jesus, fumigate and purify all aspects of my life from the smell of death and the grave and release an irresistible flavor of divine favor in my life. I cancel every appointment with death made on my behalf.

5. I resign my membership from the congregation of the dead; I declare I am offline with decay, corruption and stagnation in Jesus' mighty name.

6. I disconnect myself from the flow of evil from my family and all previous associations in Jesus' name. I command all generational evil inheritance to catch fire now in Jesus' name.

7. Every slaughter I have been experiencing because of the iniquity of my fathers has come to an end today in Jesus' name. I command the avenger of blood on ancestral altars to burn with the altars to ashes in Jesus Name.

8. I declare a new door to a new life opened unto me this day in Jesus' name.

   PSALM 16:9-11. Therefore my heart is glad, and my glory rejoiceth: my flesh also shall rest in hope.

   For thou wilt not leave my soul in hell; neither wilt thou suffer thine Holy One to see corruption.
   Thou wilt shew me the path of life: in thy presence is fulness of joy; at thy right hand there are pleasures for evermore.

9. Rejoice and give God praise.

Practical Deliverance Session

There is a compelling need to conduct deliberate and effective deliverance sessions at the earliest possible opportunity for people coming to faith in the Lord Jesus Christ. Such an early start in this important direction will help to eliminate grounds for recurrent demonic activity and spare God's people years of delay, pain, and needless frustration in their journey of faith. God's people will be empowered to walk in the liberty that the Lord Jesus Christ purchased for us through His atoning death, burial and resurrection.

There are four levels at which this may be done.

1. Group Deliverance Services

Group deliverance service is a somewhat more general form of deliverance. It is like a church service or a crusade service where the issues of demonic bondage are highlighted and people are generally taught or counseled by the Word of God. This might be followed by questions and answers, after which the deliverance minister leads the congregation in a session of warfare prayers - breaking covenants and hidden curses, and applying the Blood of Jesus. And in that corporate anointed atmosphere, the power of God is released.

This kind of general deliverance session has its own advantage in that many people can be helped under that corporate anointing. Chains get broken, yokes are removed, and healings flow freely. Such sessions, however, can be way more effective if there are deliverance team members within a given anointed structure, who have received training on how to handle people, so that when that corporate anointing is moving, people then can be assisted generally to come into liberty, and the demonic issues are cleaned up properly and thoroughly.

2. Faith Clinics
A Faith Clinic is another form of group deliverance but it is group deliverance "par excellence." This is the method often employed by specialized deliverance ministries and groups. Just as the name implies, this type of group operates like a hospital or clinic. It

combines a unique blend of deliverance emphases with an interdisciplinary pool of other ministry gifts or specializations to address the multifaceted needs of different case scenarios that otherwise might prove difficult if they were handled in the more general type of anointed atmosphere.

Typically, you would have a pool of skilled spiritual counselors, word teachers, prayer warriors, prophetic hands, seers, and support staff, all working together in a team to secure the thorough release, cleansing, and healing of the oppressed and afflicted person.

How is this done?
The leadership of the deliverance team or ministry decides on a given date to schedule a deliverance clinic. Groundwork before the date will include preparation of advertorials and questionnaires for collecting data in the counseling sessions. There should also be statements of release from legal prosecution, duly signed by those benefitting from deliverance ministrations. Such statements should be prepared by a qualified legal practitioner. Spiritual preparation includes a time of fasting, prayer, and seeking the Lord for direction and the release of His anointing of might in the coming event.

On the given date, the ministry team is broken into smaller units to give emphasis to specific areas, including the following:

(a) The registration desk, to properly log in those appearing for help. This is a good time to fill out the deliverance forms, as well as the legal release forms.

(b) There should be a general area where worship, teachings, and questions and answers are provided nonstop by the teaching unit.

(c) While this is going on, seekers are quietly picked out and assigned to skilled spiritual counselors in the counseling unit who then counsel and make notes on the deliverance forms earlier filled out by seekers.

(d) This is passed on to the prayer warrior team, among them prophets and seers, who pray through and make their own recommendations based on revelation from the Lord.

(e) By now, those casting out devils or implementing cleansing are fully ready to clear out the demon spirits and minister healing.

Keep in mind here that I am suggesting an ideal situation where you have a large pool of dedicated and trained warriors upon which to draw. This is the best case scenario and deliverance works seamlessly. However, the Lord can always find a way to do His work where people love and desire to do His will, no matter the limitations.

3. Individual Counseling Sessions

This refers to one-on-one ministry encounters between the deliverance minister and the individual seeker. In this scenario, the minister has more room because he is the one scheduling the people for ministration, and he is able to schedule one or two sessions to really counsel an individual in detail. The essence is to probe into the personal life of the average seeker, to hear their stories of struggles, to invite the searchlight of the Holy Spirit to take an introspective journey into the individual's life, and to locate underlying reasons for demonic oppression and struggles.

It is important to always remember that the Lord, the Holy Spirit, is the actual Deliverer so as to deliberately allow Him to lead and guide the process. If we allow Him, we can quickly get to the root cause of the oppression.

In the course of conducting deliverances through the years, I have found that individual counseling sessions actually offer a very unique opportunity to teach the person who is being delivered about the details of what is involved, what they are to expect, and what their responses may be for them to meaningfully participate in the process. Also, I have found that it is useful in many cases to ask the individual to go into some kind of fasting so that the Holy Spirit can show them things that they do not know but are very important as part of the strategy for their liberty.

You will get to know firsthand, as the Holy Spirit begins to unravel details of their lives and bring it to their awareness, things they did not even know or perhaps did not reckon were important to their deliverance. These things can come to us by way of divinely inspired dreams, visions, and revelations. This will make the deliverance session more direct and to the point. The individual who is receiving deliverance in this process comes to find out that the Holy Spirit is far more involved in their deliverance than the deliverance minister who is providing the help. Then they can be appropriately motivated to continue the deliverance issues on an ongoing basis with the Person of the Holy

Spirit who is actually the Deliverer. The individual counseling sessions or ministry can be the most effective.

4. Self-Deliverance

Self-Deliverance, as the name suggests, means to conduct deliverance on yourself: set yourself free and cast out the devil, using your God-given authority in the mighty name of the Lord Jesus Christ! Self-Deliverance refers to when an individual who is in some kind of demonic struggle realizes what is going on and has a measure of understanding or revelation in the Word of God, particularly in relation to our authority in Christ. The believer has authority over every devil through Jesus Christ. Even before the atoning death of our Lord Jesus Christ, He delegated this authority to his disciples to go out and preach the Gospel and to cast out devils. The Bible says that they returned again with joy, saying, "Lord, even the devils are subject unto us through thy name" (Luke 10:17-20).

"Dealing with the devil outside of our authority in Christ puts the believer in a disadvantageous position to the enemy and you can bring yourself into cheap bondage to the enemy."

Believers who have an understanding of their God-given authority in Christ Jesus can exercise that authority in self-ministrations, break demonic covenants, apply the Blood, and command the demons to be flushed out. The advantage of self-deliverance is that you are handling your deliverance between you and the Holy Spirit and things are facilitated quickly. Besides, you are able to quickly learn how to use your God-given authority to control the devil.

Actually, the only meaningful way a Christian can relate to the devil is to use his authority in Christ Jesus to control the enemy. Dealing with the devil outside of our authority in Christ puts the believer in a disadvantageous position to the enemy and you can bring yourself into bondage to the enemy. Self-deliverance actually enhances growth in that authority but a basic understanding of your authority, to begin with, is very necessary, especially realizing that the devil is subject to you in the name of Jesus. When I say the devil, I mean any category of evil spirits, from Lucifer to the smallest demon, is subject to the believer in Christ Jesus through the name of Jesus. Self-deliverance will enhance growth in the development of a believer's authority.

The flip side of self-deliverance is that if you do not have that much knowledge about your authority in Christ Jesus, or if the level of bondage is slightly on the stronger side and manifestations begin, you probably will not be able to handle it correctly. In such cases, it is good to get some help by approaching your minister or a trusted hand that is anointed and walking in God's authority to walk you through at least up to a certain extent.

ISSUES ADDRESSED IN A PRACTICAL DELIVERANCE SESSION

1. Repentance

Repentance means godly sorrow over sin, a change of mind and position regarding sins which then re-aligns us in total agreement with God. Repentance can be both direct (for personal sins) and also through identification with the misdeeds of past generations. This forms the foundation or bedrock for securing divine attention and intervention.

The person seeking deliverance must first become properly informed about the issues and doorways, both personal and generational. Repentance here means coming into agreements with the Word of God about sin, evil covenants, and demonic worship. This includes personal identification with the faulty foundation our ancestors stood upon to incur the wrath of God. We can humble ourselves in brokenness, acknowledge our sins, and accept God's offer of mercy.

Genuine repentance invites God's mercy and intervention. In Psalm 51:17, the Bible says, "The sacrifices of God are a broken spirit: a broken and a contrite heart, O God, thou wilt not despise." Repentance is like issuing an eviction notice to the devil. The Blood of Jesus is the legal ground for deliverance, but repentance is a way of telling the binding evil powers that their time is up.

2. Breaking Evil Covenants
(Renunciation, Denunciation and Revocation of Evil Covenants- applying the blood of Jesus to the root causes of demonic bondage)

Why is this necessary? The enemy, as I said earlier, really cannot bind anyone without some kind of covenant, which results from interacting with things that are controlled or engineered by the wicked. The Blood of Jesus, however, is the legal ground for liberty;

so applying the Blood of Jesus to break every hidden curse or satanic covenant, is a firm starting point.

Such covenants might be blood covenants, meal covenants, covenants enacted through sex, through dreams, through participation in occult activities, or covenants through ancestral exposures where they might have sought the help of the enemy. These and others are what the enemy uses as breeding grounds for oppression. They must be renounced and broken by the application of the Blood of Jesus.

It is important to reckon with the standing of the Blood. The Blood is the same as the very life of Jesus, the being of Jesus, the essence of Jesus. The entirety of who He is and

"Repentance is like issuing an eviction notice to the devil.... repentance is a way of telling the binding evil powers that their time is up."

what He has done is represented in His Blood. The Blood of Jesus is the highest investment on the face of the universe, as far as God's grace and power are concerned. Jesus is the Lamb of God slain from the foundation of this world. From the foundation, the Blood is already there. The Bible calls it the Blood of the

Everlasting Covenant (Hebrews 13:20).

So, through the operation of the Blood of Jesus, no matter how far or how deep or how wide satanic bondage may pretend to be, it will be broken. Even if you had dined or gone to bed with the devil, as soon as you realize that it was wrong and decide that you do not want to continue that relationship with the devil but want to serve the Living God, be set free, and walk in the liberties of the sons of God, the Blood of Jesus can be brought into that situation and the curse simply broken.

This is where Satan is really weak because even though he likes to keep people in bondage forever, he quite simply does not have the means to do so because the Blood of Jesus has broken the curse. Colossians 2:14-15 says: **"Blotting out the handwriting of ordinances that was against us, which was contrary to us, and took it out of the way, nailing it to his cross; And having spoiled principalities and powers, he made a shew of them openly, triumphing over them in it."**

The Amplified Bible (Classic Edition) puts it this way: **"Having cancelled and blotted out and wiped away the handwriting of the note (bond) with its legal** decrees and demands which was in force and stood against us (hostile to us). This [note with its regulations, decrees, and demands] He set aside and cleared completely out of our way by nailing it to [His] cross. [God] disarmed the principalities and powers that were ranged against us and made a bold display and public example of them, in triumphing over them in Him and in it [the cross]."

So through the Cross of the Lord Jesus Christ, every curse has been broken and Satan has been disarmed. His lethal weapon, his poison, which was introduced into our system, can all be cleared out by the application of the Blood.

3. Authoritative Warfare

This involves aggressive warfare and forceful confrontation of binding powers. Having eliminated the legal grounds for demonic oppression by breaking evil covenants and denouncing hidden curses, it is now time to take the battle to the evil one in warfare prayers. This is a vital step, whether in group deliverance, in individual counseling sessions, or in self-deliverance.

In aggressive warfare, we demolish the strongholds of the enemy and close the doors that may have validated the devil's illegal activity. I cannot overemphasize the fact that in this session, the Holy Spirit must be allowed to guide us. We therefore must open ourselves up to Him in worship and adoration. And, as we worship God, we move into that place of authority and begin to break the powers through the application of the Blood and warfare prayers.

Let me emphasize, one more time, that the Blood of Jesus provides the legal grounds to liquidate any liability that the enemy may be acting upon to perpetuate a situation of bondage. Prayer warfare allows us to confront the "higher ranking powers" in their demonic enclaves, base or cities and dismantle the chains at the root levels.

4. The Holy Spirit Power and House Cleaning

House cleaning involves flushing out residual demonic elements. The ground has been made ready and it is now time for the power of the Holy Spirit to move through the deliverance ministers and through the deliverance team to eliminate and cast out demons from the house. This is the part most folks are anxious to reach, but care must be taken to carefully follow the first three points above.

I want to state here that as deliverance ministers, we are to be very patient and tolerant, methodical, and deliberate. We should not come into deliverance session if we are tired and worn-out. We should come in prepared, relying on the Holy Spirit to work through us, so that the demons do not manipulate us and continue on, while we think that they are gone. We should also not be distracted by the manifestations but carefully move with the Holy Spirit to ensure a thorough clean out.

Flushing demons out of an individual is only one side of the coin but the final objective of Deliverance is discipleship. The work of deliverance does not stop in the deliverance session rather, it's only the beginning of an important but ongoing process. This brings us to the critical point that the work of deliverance is really not the work of a deliverance minister. It is the work of the Holy Spirit. God's Holy Spirit takes over from this point, particularly as the individual is taught to pay attention to His work in their own lives. Here, the person who has just received ministration must maintain fellowship with the Holy

House cleaning involves flushing out residual demonic elements.

Spirit of the Living God, within the community of believers, and other pastoral authority so that the process will be effectively and thoroughly monitored to its logical conclusion.

What do you expect after the conclusion of a deliverance session? A deep work of cleansing commences.

5. Deep inner Cleansing

Let us examine the Scriptures to understand exactly what I mean by the work of deep cleansing. The Book of 2 Corinthians 7:1 says, **"Having therefore these promises dearly beloved, let us cleanse ourselves from all filthiness of the flesh and of the spirit perfecting holiness in the fear of God."**

What promises is the writer talking about? In the preceding chapter, we are exhorted to come out from uncleanness, filthiness, and demonic pollutions, and be separated, so that God can dwell or tabernacle in us. In other words, God's promise to the believer is that He will be a mobile ark, a mobile vehicle for carrying around the very presence of God, the Divinity and Person of God. So, we are God-carriers.

This was God's original purpose for man. He made us in His image and likeness in the beginning - male and female - so that we can have dominion and exercise that dominion over His creation. That remains His purpose. What is the enemy's purpose? To reverse that order. The enemy's purpose is to dominate man, bind him, and seize his authority over all creation. In order to do this, the demons open an individual up to gain access. Thereafter, they begin to reproduce their evil nature in the person. This individual grows up thinking that the evil nature of the demon is their own personality.

Just imagine how many people think that they were born to be homosexuals simply because they feel that way! God does not create anyone to be a homosexual; it is the demonic infiltration of man that creates such conditions. And once you start accepting and validating it, by claiming 'that's the way you are,' you become what you say you are because the demon is then able to completely take you over.

"Any compulsive behavior that we have acquired over time that makes us feel helpless to control our desires is because of demonic corruption that has taken over our human personality."

This goes for all things that are contrary to sound doctrine that people embrace - whether it is fornication, lying, stealing, or adultery. Any compulsive behavior that we have acquired over time that makes us feel helpless to control our desires is because of demonic corruption that has taken over our human personality. Demons enter to reproduce their evil natures. An individual may look at certain aspects of their character and say "I am out of control, completely helpless." These are demonic issues. What the Lord wants to do is to effect the work of deep inner cleansing and reconfiguration.

6. The Word of God and Cleansing

There is a work of the Holy Spirit that ensues from the initial deliverance session. He goes to work and arranges every circumstance and begins to apply the Word of the Living God. This is why teaching and discipleship in the Word of God is a major issue of concern to me. If you and I are going to walk in liberty, we do not have an alternative to the Word of God. The Word of God will clean us up. The Bible says, "How can a young

"The Word of God recaptures grounds that the enemy has stolen in our soul realm and begins to reconfigure them."

man cleanse his way? By taking heed according to your word" (Psalm 119:9).

The Word of God cleanses. How does this happen? The Word of God recaptures grounds that the enemy has stolen in our soul realm and begins to reconfigure them. The Bible refers to this as renewal or reprogramming. The Word of the Living God reprograms us. Why do we need to be reprogrammed? So that we can be harmonized with Divinity. Demonic pollution, possession, and infestation have one objective, and that is to configure us into the devil's image. If you are reconfigured in the devil's image, you automatically belong to him, and he does not only take residence in you, he works hard to make sure you end up in hell with him in eternity.

Why was the Word of God given to us? To reconfigure us, so that our nature becomes harmonized with Divinity, and we become like God in character and in nature. The more we become like God, the more demons will actually fear, hate, and flee from us. That is why as soon as a believer starts walking in the image of God, the devil will start to blackmail them, persecute them, and generally fight them; but if we stay in the

Word, fellowship, and accountability, the Word continues to work from deep within us.

Most of the compulsive behaviors and attitudes that people cannot seem to control, whether it be emotions of anger or perverted emotions of love (that function and fester as uncontrollable, lustful desires for things or people) or some lewd or unnatural desires and vile affections, have been programmed by the enemy through the years. The Word of God can go to the root of these behaviors and begin to work a cleansing, a restructuring, a reprogramming from within, and with time, people will come into real liberty.

This is how to achieve meaningful deliverance. This is why Jesus said to those who believed on Him: **"If ye continue in My Word, then are ye My disciples indeed; And ye shall know the truth, and the truth shall make you free"** (John 8:30-32).

The Word of God will restructure, revamp, and reconfigure areas in the human soul or character that have been demonized, bound or corrupted, so that this person will achieve total wholeness. Inner healing and wholeness is the final objective of cleansing. The more we look at the Word, the more we become the Word. We become a marvel to ourselves and to others. This is true deliverance.

Let me make this point very clear. The desire to just experience

"Demonic pollution, possession, and infestation have one objective, and that is to configure us into the devil's image. If you are configured in the devil's image, you automatically belong to him, and he does not only take residence in you, he works hard to make sure you end up in hell in eternity with him."

temporary freedom from constraints without a corresponding commitment to walk the path of discipleship is recycled bondage, not deliverance. It is wrong for deliverance ministers to make the process more confusing by emphasizing only the material benefits that come from deliverance. The benefits are real, but excessive emphasis on them cheapens the whole objective of deliverance; and those who are participating in the deliverance soon find out that they are in endless cycles.

I would suggest to anyone seeking deliverance that you go to a deliverance ministry and get some help (if necessary), but stay in a local church that focuses on the Word of God. I say this with a sense of responsibility. People who congregate in what is called "deliverance ministries" cannot grow because most deliverance ministries are not equipped to truly disciple people to become strong in the Word of God. The reason is this: the anointing of deliverance is an aspect of the working of miracles. Working of miracles is in the realm of the ministry of an evangelist. The gift of faith, the gift of healing, and the working of miracles are all in the realm of the ministry of an evangelist. So, even if it is an apostolic evangelist that is equipped to start a church and start mobilizing masses of people, those people cannot be established in the grace of God without the Word of God.

"The desire to just experience temporary freedom from constraints without a corresponding commitment to walk the path of discipleship is recycled bondage, not deliverance."

FIND A TEACHING MINISTRY AND CONNECT

A teaching ministry will do far more good particularly for people who have gone through demonic circumstances. I will go even further to say a teaching ministry, with emphasis on faith, will help you even faster, and especially if you had been in an occult background or occult church but have now come into deliverance. If you decide to stay in a deliverance ministry forever, you will not go beyond the basics. Very quickly, the enemy can move in on you and begin to cripple your life. And that is why you find that people can be in "deliverance ministries' for years and their lives are not moving anywhere.

You cannot get people together and continue to teach about witchcraft endlessly. People cannot be strong in faith by that type of knowledge. The just shall live by faith! Faith in the Word of God is the ticket for daily living. And this is why faith teachers must not lose their bite. New creation teachers must not lose their bite because the people of God need the Word of God.

The Flip Side

On the flip side, however, faith teachers and new creation teachers oftentimes presume a lot about deliverance ministry. They believe that in Christ you are already delivered. Actually, this is true, in a way. In

Christ, you are delivered, but there is something called deliverance or cleansing from demonic infestations. There is something called deep bondage that merely

> *"Inner healing and wholeness is the final objective of cleansing. The more we look at the Word of God, the more we become the Word."*

responding to an altar call doesn't resolve. The Word of God is the major instrument of deliverance. Everything hangs on it. Everything stands on and falls on the Word of God. All creation, the whole universe, is hanging on the Word of God. Even the devil himself does not have a reality outside of the Word of God; so he is subject to the Word of God. That said, we still counsel people and do some warfare for many to enjoy real liberty.

I really do not know how much I can emphasize this truth. There is no deliverance without the Word of God. And, if I may say this also, if people obey the Word, no matter what the kind of bondage may be there at the beginning, if they continue to obey the Word of God, that bondage will break; it will snap. The deliverance anointing is an extra layer of help that God has brought to the end-time church to promote cleansing, wholeness and reclaiming of lost inheritances, so that the church can come into the full blessing and do the work of ministry.

7. The Fear of the Lord and Cleansing

Another important consideration in effecting deep cleansing is knowledge of and correct response to the fear of the Lord. The Bible says, **"Having therefore these promises, dearly beloved, let us cleanse ourselves from all filthiness of the flesh and spirit, perfecting holiness in the fear of God"** (2 Corinthians 7:1). Two things are outlined here. First is cleansing ourselves of pollutions of the spirit and the flesh (these are the two levels of pollution). The second thing is to mature in holiness or completeness out of reverence for God.

Remember, when the Bible talks about deliverance in the Book of Obadiah, it says, **"But upon Mount Zion shall be deliverance, and there shall be holiness; and the house of Jacob shall possess their possessions"** (1:17). Holiness, as I said earlier, is wholeness, completeness. God is holy because He is absolutely complete lacking in nothing. So, holiness is not only in the sense of moral purity, but it is also in terms of completeness in all that we are meant to be, so that we can do all what we are called to do. God is completely whole, so He can meet any need. That is why He said **"upon Mount Zion shall be holiness and the sons of Jacob shall possess their possession."** Deliverance is connected to your inheritance.

How the Fear of the Lord helps us

How, practically speaking here, does the fear of the Lord help us? Let me explain it to you this way. When demons live in somebody, they reproduce their evil nature, particularly in things that are addictive. Anything that has an addictive element is fastened by demonic forces in the mind. Here is an example. I once worked among drug addicts in Nigeria and noticed that addiction has two levels. The first level is the psychological, or the mind. The second level deals with the physical side, the body.

Take for instance, an addict who is using a particular drug of choice which he enjoys. When he takes that drug, sensations in the central nervous system are triggered and feelings of pleasure are generated, but they are short-lived. What causes addiction therefore is the desire to repeat those initial pleasurable experiences. The addicted person wants to feel euphoria, so he takes the drug again but finds out that he needs increasing doses of the same drug to get the high. So he keeps doing that, but while he is at it, another level of bondage is occurring. Besides the mind being captured, the physical body is also becoming adjusted, or tolerant to the drug to the point that, after sometime, the body becomes chemically dependent on that drug and cannot function without it.

Now, there are two problems the person's mind is captured he wants to repeat the feeling; and the body is adjusted, or addicted, or dependent on the chemical and he cannot function without the chemical. If he withdraws the chemical, he goes into painful withdrawal symptoms. Now, the addicted person has two motivations. He wants the feeling but also fears the pain that withdrawal can bring on; therefore he is in hot pursuit of the drug.

Demons hide their evil intentions
Behind attractive images

The devil works exactly the same way. He might trigger some behavior or behavioral malady by first encouraging someone to engage in some type of illicit pleasurable behavior. While they are doing that, he captures the mind. And, after a while, he enters their body and adjusts the body and begins to reproduce the conditions.

So, the devil is not only in the mind, he is also in the body. When you cast him out through a deliverance session, the job would have just started because the devil is going to continue to trigger certain pictures in the mind of the individual. As he triggers those pictures in the mind, the body starts to react. If people are not trained in the Word of God, after enduring those hallucinations and haunting pictures, feelings are going to be triggered in their body to move and their wills will be broken. And that is why some people are in a trap. To break the power of the enemy, you have to deal with that image.

A character in a Chinese movie I watched some time ago said something quite instructive. He said that the enemy hides its intentions behind images. To break the power of the enemy, you have to find the image and break it. What is the image? The pleasure you are seeking to have; that thing you cannot do without. The enemy hides behind it. So, if you cast out a demon from someone, it is just relief. The image is still there, and it is only the Word of God and the fear of God that can correct it.

Where does the fear of God come in? When you have just gone through a deliverance session, the demons are cleaned out of you. However, because your body system had over time adjusted to the behaviors triggered by the demons, the Word of God takes you through a process of reclaiming and revamping. For this process to succeed, you have to have a level of respect for God.

When you are alone in a place and nobody is watching you, you will be tempted to do certain things. You will be tempted to go to certain places. It takes only the fear or respect you have for God to prevent you from doing these things. This is why the Psalmist says "the fear of the Lord is clean, enduring forever" (Psalm 19:9). The fear of the Lord is a spiritual antiseptic that will clean your life from contamination with evil. If you do not have the fear of the Lord and a commitment to discipleship in the Word of God, deliverance is a nonstarter.

Think of it this way. How comfortable would you be as a believer, who is going through a deliverance process, if most of the things you agree to do when no one is watching were to be played on public television? Well, you may consider this as a mere hypothetical allusion, but the fact is that the things you engage in are all on the monitors of heaven. And if these activities are ungodly and immoral, the angels are being embarrassed, and God is forced to look at these things, which is a great dishonor to Him.

So, the fear in 2 Corinthians 7:1 actually refers to a deep personal reverence for your Father in heaven. If you respect God, you will not subject Him to the harrowing experience of looking at you down here once again giving yourself, your body, to work wickedness. Why would you engage anymore in immoral behavior? Because nobody is watching you, or you think God will understand? Well, God understood enough to put His Son on the Cross in order to save us from a burning hell so, why not obey the Word of God?

People need a little respect for God particularly in this perverted and crooked generation where the preachers of the Gospel of love are making people lose their sense

PRACTICAL DELIVERANCE SESSION

PRACTICAL DELIVERANCE SESSION

of responsibility and accountability. You have to make a choice. The fear of the Lord comes by choice. It is something you choose. If you choose *"The fear of the Lord is a spiritual antiseptic that will clean your life from contamination with evil."* to fear the Lord, then His fear will be in you, and His fear will protect, defend, and keep you clean from contamination with evil. God says in His Word, **"A son honoureth his father, and a servant his master: if then I be a father, where is mine honor? And if I be a master, where is my fear? saith the LORD of hosts unto you, O priests, that despise my name. And ye say, wherein have we despised thy name?" (Malachi 1:6).**

You and I have to make that choice. It is by choice we love our Father and show appreciation for the great work of salvation, the tremendous privilege of deliverance, cleansing, and wholeness. But we certainly do not intend to continue to cohabit with the devil so that grace will abound more and more. No, we are a delivered people and we are a determined people also. We are an accountable people who are committed to walk the Word of God and leave no room for Satan's bondage.

BENEFITS OF SPIRITUAL CLEANSING

What is the benefit of this level of spiritual cleansing?

1. Freedom

Firstly, it is very rewarding to be free indeed! Just to be able to look at Satan's addictive behavior that once held you bound and robbed you of personal dignity; just to be able to look at it in the face and say, *I am not there anymore. I was once a fornicator but I'm not anymore. I was a cheat but I'm not anymore. I was a compulsive liar but I am not anymore. I was a slave to some demons who could ride me at will, but I am not anymore.* It is so liberating! Praise the Living God!

2. A Definite Promise

Secondly, God made a promise. **"Wherefore come out from among them, and be ye separate, saith the Lord, and touch not the unclean thing; and I will receive you, And will be a Father unto you, and ye shall be my sons and daughters, saith the Lord Almighty" (2 Corinthians 6:17-18).** Think of it! As the enemy is kept out of our lives, room is made for God to fill us. When I carry God, when I carry His love, His nature when I carry His authority, I will go out there and begin to victimize the same devil that once victimized me before.

3. Regain your Inheritance

Thirdly, the Bible says when we are delivered and embrace the Holy Spirit, we are empowered to receive our possessions or our inheritance. Many of God's children are groaning under bondage; the enemy wants to keep them shackled because they represent the hope of their families. There are certain levels of blessings and increase that God wants to give His people, and if we allow God to transmit this inheritance to us, we will become the showcase of our generation, the hope of our families and the hope of the church.

In other words, if God is given the opportunity by you and me to really bring us into His full glory and the full measure of blessings He has for us, then we automatically become blessings. Consequently, when we appear on the scene, poverty bows out; when we appear on the scene, sickness bows out; when we appear on the scene, family dignity is restored and enhanced. As our families gather around the light that we now have from God, they will receive help; our children and our parents will be blessed; and our generation will smile because we are here. All of these the enemy is working hard to prevent by trying to bind and ridicule us. But bless the Lord that the Holy Spirit is helping the church this day!

4. Live out your Destiny

Another benefit of accepting God's help and true deliverance is that you would truly have embraced your destiny. The Bible says that we are going to be the repairer of many generations and be called the priests of our God (Isaiah 61:4). Instead of laboring under a generational curse, you are actually unleashing and perpetuating generational blessings. You are the curse-breaker in the family; you bring an end to the pain and the shame, and you unleash generational blessings so that those coming after you will not have to struggle under the yoke. You make a difference, a positive difference.

WHEN DEMONS ARE EXPELLED

I want to mention some things you might see in the process of cleansing. As the initial process of cleansing commences, there may be manifestations or there may not be. When I say manifestations, I mean strong manifestations during prayers like falling, foaming at the mouth, phlegm being coughed up, and so on, when the power of God hits and the enemy is coming out.

For some people, during the cleansing process, continuous flow of sputum might set in lasting several days or more. If this happens, do not be embarrassed; just go through it. For others, as they are reading the Bible, they may constantly yawn or tear up. These are cleansing processes and the person should not be embarrassed. And for some others, depending on the severity of what they were involved in, this period of cleansing and breaking covenant can open up bizarre dream experiences. Those who go through this level of reaction should seek close monitoring from experienced and trained deliverance counselors.

Dreaming is an important gateway into the spirit realm. In your dream state, depending on how or where you were before, or even the nature of your family background, you might have all kinds of experiences. The first line of defense for you is to read the Word of God. I call it Word Therapy. Saturate your mind with the Word, because your mind is a gateway into your spirit. If the Word of God is not guarding your mind, then deliverance becomes a total failure and your spirit becomes an open expressway to all kinds of demonic influences and manipulations.

So, the first line of defense is just doing Word Therapy. Word Therapy means that you are not necessarily studying but you are just reading several chapters to bombard your mind with the Word of God. That cleanses your mind and reprograms your mind and resets your mind so that the enemy's manipulative strategies become ineffective to a great extent.

"If the Word of God is not guarding your mind, then deliverance becomes a total failure and your spirit becomes an open expressway to all kinds of demonic influences and manipulations."

Secondly, you should, if possible, seek close monitoring or mentoring from an experienced deliverance counselor, more especially one that has a prophetic vein and can interpret dreams and is able to decode the source of dreams, because not all dreams come from God.

I explained a lot about dreams in my book, *"Prophetic Gateways,"* but let me mention here that there are three types of dreams that can come to you:

(1) Dreams that come from God called divine revelations;

(2) dreams that come from yourself manifestations of your state; and

(3) dreams that come from the devil manipulations. This third category of dreams is the one to most watch out for when you have gone through deliverance prayers.

Manipulation is the enemy swinging on the other extreme. There are two ways the enemy functions:

(1) He wants people to think that he does not exist; this way, he can destroy quietly without being detected.

(2) He wants people to know that he exists but passes himself off as being so relevant or powerful that nothing can be done about him, which of course, is a lie. He is a creature, and a fallen one at that. He has lost his original position with God, so he cannot even maintain the originality of his power. He is a fading power, which is another topic as to how the devil is able to maintain his power on the earth. Suffice it is to say that he is a bloody creature, which is why he triggers a lot of violence

on the earth to generate blood to sustain his demonic activities.

What is the sign that you are being manipulated by dreams? Hopelessness! Any time you are being manipulated in your dream, you feel hopeless. Anything that makes you feel hopeless is not from God. It is an antichrist spirit. Even when God is rebuking His children, He will generate faith and hope. Anything that neutralizes your faith and removes your hope is demonic. Fear, hopelessness, and faithlessness are the hallmarks to indicate that there is demonic manipulation going on.

PEOPLE COMING OUT OF AN OCCULT BACKGROUND

I have a special message for those coming from an occult environment, particularly occult-based "churches." I say occult-based churches because there are so-called churches that are not founded on the Word of God. They are syncretic with a mixture of the Word and occult practices. These are churches that are founded by people who had an encounter with Christianity but were not really born-again and cleansed from an existing demonic or occult background. Thus, the enemy manipulates them into thinking they are hearing from God and they go on to start churches and organizations that are syncretic.

Syncretism results from a mixture of the previous occult foundation through visions, illusions, manipulations of the enemy and then trying to teach the Bible. This constitutes two opposites coming together. If people come from that kind of church environment, where there is usually much emphasis on visions and dreams, the enemy will seek to perpetuate that when you come to faith.

The just shall live by faith (Hebrews 10:38). This was why I emphasized earlier on that the faith teachers of our day and age would do the church of Jesus Christ an injustice if they do not teach the faith message. The faith message is critical. Why? The Bible says the just shall live by faith. And as we are entering the end zone of the end time, there is a much more upsurge of occult phenomena trying to penetrate authentic Christianity. If the faith message is lost, we will be in trouble.

And as I would say to every person who is reading these lines, invest in materials that teach on faith. For example, the writings of the late Kenneth Hagin on faith will help you. Get hold of faith-building materials and build up your faith. Faith in the Word of God is an important foundation. The Bible does not say the just shall live by dreams or by visions or by prophecies. I stand in the prophetic office but I will say to you, you cannot live by prophets. You only live by the Word of God.

There are so many people who congregate in meetings, wanting a prophet to prophesy to them. Even though I operate in the prophetic office, I do not like this because I know that commitment to prophets, visions, and revelations often neutralizes the faith of the people. Faith is to be in the Living Word of God. Read that Word. Get some faith materials, build your faith. In your daily fight against the devil, you need your faith.

It takes faith in the Word of God to function in the required authority. With God, you relate with faith and submission. With man, you relate with conscience. But with the devil, you need your authority. If anything affects your authority, you become beggarly. That is why faith is so important. The just shall live by faith, not by dreams!

BREAKTHROUGH PROPHETIC DELIVERANCE PRAYERS

1. Precious Holy Spirit my Deliverer and Counselor, unveil every hidden satanic undercurrents and enabling character deficiency in my life; and like a mighty River, visit me and mobilize a new standard in me that the evil one cannot handle.

2. Lord God, I invite you to correct every area of contradiction in my character due to demonic corruption and implement a deep work of cleansing within me in the Mighty Name of the Lord Jesus Christ.

3. I reverently submit myself to the working and washing of your Word. Let your Holy Word work within me and abide in me until I become one with your Word. Reconcile and harmonize any violated parts of my soul to yourself in the mighty Name Jesus Christ.

4. I confess and declare here and now that I am the righteousness of God in Christ Jesus and that every devil is subject to me in the Mighty Name of my Lord and Savior Jesus Christ.

5. Lord God of glory, I this day commit to honor you in my life and personally chose your Fear over the fear of evil. I reverently submit myself to you and commit to shun every evil way and instead keep myself in your love. I will abide in your love forever my God in the mighty Name of Jesus Christ.

CHAPTER

3

Three Days of Deliverance Prayer with Fasting

There is spiritual significance to three days. In the Old Testament, God would often command His people to consecrate themselves for three days before His visitation and blessing.

Exodus 19:10-11, for example, says: **"And the LORD said unto Moses, Go unto the people, and sanctify them today and tomorrow, and let them wash their clothes, And be ready against the third day: for the third day the LORD will come down in the sight of all the people upon Mount Sinai."**

The Lord Jesus defeated eternal death and brought immortality to life in three days. There is something very special when we wait upon the Lord in a three-day fasting and prayer retreat for deliverance. This can also be a seven, fourteen or even twenty-one-day deliverance fast, but a three-day fast can effectively unleash resurrection glory and allow the Lord the opportunity to get to the root of binding powers and dislodge them.

I have a lot of personal testimonies in my life and the lives of others resulting from a three-day shut in with the Lord for personal release and blessing.

PREPARATION TO START A THREE-DAY SHUT IN

1. Before you are due to start fasting, begin to make a faith presentation of yourself to God for grace to rest upon you in the fast (Romans 12:1-2). Present or commit your fast ahead to Him before you begin to receive even more grace to complete the fast.

2. While preparing to start, continue in counseling with your deliverance minister and write all dreams and revelations you might have along the way.

3. It is time to agree on the set date and location with your minister. Once the date is set, have a determination to follow through as the devil will

fight hard to distract and stop the deliverance session from happening; he is merely making a play for survival. You should have an iron-clad determination to follow through even if you fall sick in the process. If you stay on the plan, God's grace will kick in. Remember, the Lord Himself is watching and monitoring the entire process.

4. Have a final counseling session to review observations, dreams, revelations, recollections and draw up a working list of items to address in prayer warfare for the three days.

DAY ONE

1. Avoid distractions
Arrive a night, preferably before, to minimize distractions. Turn off your phone and cut off the internet, television, and social media interactions.

2. Immerse yourself in worship
Don't be overwhelmed. You are in your Father's presence and will leave there changed. Start out with Thanksgiving and appreciate Him.

3. Repentance

Repentance means godly sorrow over sin and a change of mind and position regarding sins, which then re-aligns us in total agreement with God. Repentance can be both direct (for personal sins) and also through identification with the misdeeds of past generations. This type of repentance forms the foundation or bedrock for securing divine attention and intervention.

The person seeking deliverance must first become properly informed about the issues and doorways, both personal and generational. Repentance here means coming into agreement with the Word of God about sin, evil covenants, and demonic worship. This includes personal identification with the faulty foundation our ancestors stood upon to incur the wrath of God. We can humble ourselves in brokenness, acknowledge our sins, and accept God's offer of mercy.

Genuine repentance invites God's mercy and intervention. Psalm 51:17 (Amplified) says, "**My sacrifice acceptable to God is a broken spirit; a broken and a contrite heart (broken down with sorrow for sin and humbly and thoroughly penitent), such, O God, you will not despise.**" Repentance is like giving an eviction notice to the devil. The Blood of Jesus is the legal ground for deliverance, but repentance is telling the binding evil powers that their time is up.

4. Applying the Blood of Jesus (Renunciation, Denunciation, and Revocation of Evil Covenants)

Why is this necessary? The enemy, as I said earlier, really cannot bind anyone without some kind of covenant, which results from interacting with things that are controlled or engineered by the wicked. The Blood of Jesus, however, is the legal ground for liberty; so applying the Blood of Jesus to break every hidden curse and the satanic covenant is a firm starting point. Such covenants might be blood covenants, meal covenants, covenants enacted through sex, dreams, or participation in occult activities. They could be covenants through ancestral exposures where they might have sought the help of the enemy. These and others are what the enemy uses as breeding grounds for oppression and should be renounced and broken by the application of the Blood of Jesus.

It is important to reckon with the standing of the Blood. The Blood is the same as the life – the very life of Jesus. The being of Jesus, the essence of Jesus, the entirety of who He is and what he has done is represented in His

Blood. The Blood of Jesus is the highest investment on the face of the universe as far as God's grace and power are concerned. Jesus is the Lamb of God slain from the foundation of this world. From the foundation, the blood is already there. The Bible calls it the Blood of the Everlasting Covenant. So, through the operation of the Blood of Jesus, no matter how far, how deep, how wide satanic bondage may pretend to represent, the Blood of Jesus will break the curse.

Even if you died or went to bed with the devil, as soon as you realize that this is wrong and decide to discontinue your romance with the devil so as to serve the Living God and walk in the liberties of the sons of God, the Blood of Jesus can be brought into that situation and the curse will be broken. This is where Satan is really weak because even though he likes to keep people in bondage perpetually, he quite simply does not have the means to do so because the Blood of Jesus has broken the curse. Colossians 2:14-5 says:

> **"Blotting out the handwriting of ordinances that was against us, which was contrary to us, and took it out of the way, nailing it to his cross; And having spoiled principalities and powers, he**

**made a shew of them openly,
triumphing over them in it."**

This is how the Amplified Version puts it:

**Having cancelled and blotted out, and
wiped away the handwriting of note
(bond) with its legal decrees and
demands which was enforced and stood
against us, that is hostile to us, this note
with its regulations, decrees and
demands he set aside and cleared
completely out the way by nailing it to
his cross. God thereby disarmed the
principalities that were arranged
against us and made a bold display and
public example of them in triumphing
over them in it and on the cross."**

So through the Blood of the Lord Jesus Christ, every
curse has been broken, and Satan has been disarmed.
His lethal weapon, his poison, which was introduced
into our system, can all be cleared out by the application
of the Blood.

DAY TWO

Worship

1. Deep Worship

Worship purifies the heart of unidentified rebellions. It also brings you in complete alignment with your Victory in Christ. Remember there is absolutely no need to be tensed. You are in your Father's presence to be cleansed, empowered and blessed.

2. Authoritative Warfare

This involves the application of the Blood of Jesus to the root causes of bondage. Having eliminated the legal grounds for demonic oppression, by breaking evil covenants and denounced hidden curses, it is now time to take the battle to the evil one in warfare prayers. This is a vital step, whether in group deliverance, in individual counseling sessions, or in self-deliverance.

In aggressive warfare, we demolish the strongholds of the enemy and close the doors that may have validated the devil's illegal activity. I cannot over-emphasize the fact that in this session the Holy Spirit must be allowed to guide us. We, therefore, must open ourselves up to the Holy Spirit in worship and in adoration, and as we worship God, we move into that place of authority and begin to break the powers through the application of the Blood. Let me emphasize it one more time that the Blood of Jesus provides the legal grounds to liquidate any liability that the enemy may be acting upon to perpetuate a situation of bondage. Prayer warfare allows us to confront the stronger forces in their demonic enclaves, base or cities and dismantle the chains at the root levels.

DAY THREE

Time to Cast Them Out

1. Review your dreams and revelations. Make a note of them and utilize them in your prayers.

2. If you are implementing self-deliverance, command the demons to come out and leave. You are likely to sense some movement in your lower abdominal or throat areas; do not be alarmed. Keep commanding the demons to leave and breathe in and out. If you are receiving help directly from a deliverance worker or counselor, it could even speed things up; just follow instructions and do not be alarmed.

WHAT CAN HAPPEN WHEN DEMONS ARE EXITING

This will depend upon a number of factors, chief among them being where you are in your deliverance, meaning if you have done this before or not. I want to emphasize that regardless of where you are in your walk with God, you can still benefit to a large extent from deliverance exercises if you can humble yourself before the Lord without presuming that nothing can be wrong.

The following may be observed when demons are leaving:

a. *Coughing* - ranging from a dry cough to coughing up a lot of phlegm.

b. *Blowing air from your mouth or nostrils* (spirits are breath).

c. *Spitting or foaming at the mouth continuously.*

d. *Foul smells.* Some demons can generate a very foul smell when exiting. If they are as bad as they smell (which of course they are) then you want to get rid of them fast. The devils really stink!

e. *Falling and rolling.* The demons might try to knock you down; if this happens, control them, using the authority of the Name of Jesus. Remember always that the devil is subject to you through the name of the Lord Jesus Christ. If you have difficulty with this, get some help from an anointed believer or minister.

f. *Yawning and tearing.* You might be yawning and tearing up while undergoing deliverance as the demons leave. This happens to me from time to time just reading my Bible. Oh, the glory of His presence! I acknowledge His rich mercies and take everything He offers for my benefit with joy and appreciation. Thank you blessed Holy Spirit.

g. *The deliverance worker.* The deliverance worker should please be informed that the demons will try every trick in the book to try and survive the onslaught against them. As a last desperate measure, the types of demons you are about to cast out especially the ruling demon may try to attack you days before the deliverance session. This could actually be a giveaway to a discerning deliverance worker because you can know what you are dealing with in part, based on what is coming against you!

THE MUCH LONGER FAST

The much longer fast means that which could take up to seven, fourteen, twenty-one or forty days. It provides a great opportunity to put the flesh out of the way. This type of fast could be a partial one (which may involve skipping dinner, taking only liquid or vegetables, etc.) or it could be a complete one (in which only water is taken).

The same approach of the three-day fasting deliverance mentioned above are the effective areas to look out for in the longer fast. That said, the individual seeker will be able to draw heavily from revelation prayers peculiar to the longer fast. In the longer fast, the Holy Spirit unveils from day to day, the things that really need to be dealt with.

BREAKTHROUGH PROPHETIC DELIVERANCE PRAYERS

Romans 12:1-2
Therefore, I urge you, brothers and sisters, in view of God's mercy, to offer your bodies as a living sacrifice,

holy and pleasing to God—this is your true and proper worship. [2] Do not conform to the pattern of this world, but be transformed by the renewing of your mind. Then you will be able to test and approve what God's will is—his good, pleasing and perfect will.

1. Eternal and Living God, I here and now present my spirit, soul and body to you as a living sacrifice. Sanctify me by fire. Cleanse, purify and use me.

2. Lead me on the path of total deliverance and cleansing from all contamination of spirit and the flesh. Write your name on every path of my being today in the mighty name of Jesus.

OVERCOMING DELAY FACTORS IN DELIVERANCE

Why Deliverance Cases Delay

POORLY IDENTIFIED BACKGROUND ISSUES

"And you hath he quickened, who were dead in trespasses and sins; Wherein in time past ye walked according to the course of this world, according to the prince of the power of the air, the spirit that now worketh in the children of disobedience: Among whom also we all had our conversation in times past in the lusts of our flesh, fulfilling the desires of the flesh and of the mind; and were by nature the children of wrath, even as others" (Ephesians 2:1-3).

There are many factors why some deliverance cases seem to go on without results. One of such factors is the failure to reckon with the history of the individual. People have a record, and sometimes, to one degree or other, the enemy is involved in their past. You cannot completely understand what is required for an individual case to succeed if you fail to reckon with the history of the person. Listed below are some important points to consider.

1. Previous Occult Involvement

Previous involvement with the devil, especially in the occult, can present real difficulties. This can occur if an individual had related with the devil directly and benefited from him. This may sound surprising, but it is, in fact, the case with many individuals who have come to Christ and needed deliverance. They had been involved with the devil, and the devil had benefited them before. Now that they have come to Christ, the enemy wants to take back what he once gave to them and begins to fight. Thus, a period of reverses may set in for them. This requires careful consideration and handling if success is to be achieved.

There are also people who have a background with the devil; that is to say, a family history through the generations that were servants of the devil. In other words, they carry satanic authority. He might have made them influential or had given them the power to do things for themselves and him. When such a person comes to Christ from that kind of background, the devil will fight and try to tag him on the former agreement. But with careful help and determination, God will bring them through.

Some persons have been deeply corrupted by the devil while they sojourned with him. Those seeds of corruption have to be identified and dealt with. I will be more specific and detailed with that when I start to look at points of contact. Moreover, in the course of using the devil's power to advance purposes for themselves or their family, some individuals might have been waiting next in line to carry on the program the devil had in place for their family; but before they can actually step into such program, the Lord comes across them and brings them to faith. Because of that program that the enemy had for them, he is going to fight to try to have his way. So, an understanding is required, plus determination. This is why I say that in deliverance cases, the individual really has to be well integrated into the community of faith.

Many people today have a shopping list for pastors but they themselves are not ready to endure the demands of true discipleship. Yet, in reality, pastoral authority, discipline, accountability, and of course, support is required in some of these types of cases to have a real sustained breakthrough.

2. Misunderstanding of the Deliverance Process

Another reason for a delay in some deliverance cases is a lack of understanding of the deliverance process. As I wrote in a previous chapter, there is a process whereby God delivers. To everything, there is a process. For instance, in farming, there is a process of planting the seed, and watching it die, grow, mature, and bring forth a harvest. Similarly, there is a process for having a baby – conception, pregnancy for nine months, in most cases, and during that time, the baby is adjusting to the mother, the mother is adjusting to the baby, and the family is preparing for the new arrival.

In the same way, there is nothing like drive-through deliverance. There is a process. You have to understand what that process entails and what is required for each segment of that process to succeed in order to really get the best from what God is doing. Read more about this from Chapter Two in my book, "Foundations for True and Complete Deliverance."

3. Impatience and Distractions

Impatience and distractions come up because the individual who is seeking deliverance is focusing majorly on the problems or the demonic oppression or affliction, instead of trying to find out what God is doing in his or her life regarding the problem so that he or she can meaningfully cooperate with Him.

If you do not pay attention to or find out what God is doing regarding your case, you are unlikely to be able to participate meaningfully in the process. The psalmist says, **I regard the work of your hand, the operations of your hand; therefore thou shalt build me up** (Psalms 8:3). This means there are people who do not regard or pay attention to the operation of the Hand of God.

The Lord, through the Holy Spirit (Hand of God), is doing something in you. If you do not find it out and cooperate with Him, you will become impatient and distracted, hopping around, thinking that your answers will come from men and women of God.

It is true that God uses men and women who are trained and consecrated to help us but those individuals are not the deliverers. The Deliverer is the Lord Jesus Christ, and the Lord Jesus Christ in your life is represented by the Lord, the Holy Spirit. If you give attention to the Holy Spirit, men and women of God will still play their role. They will encourage you, pray for you, and counsel you but you will mostly enjoy the activity of the Holy Spirit who will perfect your deliverance.

CASE OF A DIFFICULT PREGNANCY

At this point, I want to reference a case in Genesis 25, where a woman who has had a delay in childbearing for twenty-two years finally gets pregnant. But then, at a point in the pregnancy, she notices that there is a battle going on inside her womb. Think of it. She has had twenty-two years without a baby; now that she is pregnant, a battle constantly rages in her womb. So she goes to inquire of the Lord, and the prophet of God tells her, "Inside your womb are two manners of people. One shall be stronger than the other and the elder shall serve the younger."

Now every time she feels the fighting, the rumbling in her stomach, she just smiles, and says, "Oh, these people are at it again." She is not troubled. But if she had not gotten that understanding, she would have been troubled and might have started going to all kinds of places. She might have even gone to some wrong places and have the pregnancy aborted.

This is what often happens to people because they lack an understanding of the deliverance process. They do not connect with the Holy Spirit. They just rely on different prophets and deliverance ministers; they hop-around and are not established anywhere. They are not under discipline, not under commitment, not under accountability, and not surprisingly for many of such people, the devil manages to keep certain kinds of sin in their lives through which he further reinforces himself.

Again, understanding the deliverance process and connecting with God will help to reduce the delay and give quicker results.

4. Failure to Reckon with the Three Stages of Deliverance

There are three stages in the deliverance process, each requiring a different approach: Stage One is when we come to Christ, become born-again, and then discover there are some demonic activities needing to be cleared from our lives. Curses can then be broken, while evil covenants are renounced through the prayer of deliverance and the initial cleansing is done. This is where people fall down, throw up, yawn, and spit, cough up phlegm, and other kinds of manifestations. As I said before, this is just the initial relief.

Following this is Stage Two of the deliverance process which involves warfare prayers. All these processes are important as part of God's strategies, all working together for our good. The second level is all warfare where you are taught how to pray. For good measure, there are many wonderful ministries that are teaching the Body of Christ today on spiritual warfare – how to take authority, and how to bind the enemy. This is crucial because at the initial stage we are dealing with demons in the individual. But the principalities do not really stay in a person's body; it is the lower classes of demons that seek embodiment and work in that direction.

During warfare, we are able to take the battle further to the demonic territory, to the demonic base, and as warfare prayer is going on, the power of God, the lightning of God, the arrow of God, and the sword of the Spirit, are going forth, cutting off things at the base level. Indeed, the greater the warfare, the greater the victory for the people of God.

However, this warfare also has some implications. When you begin to do warfare prayers, typically, you are hitting the demonic authorities at the control base. When this warfare intensifies, the principalities become affected, and so they want to find out, *"What's going on here? We had this person bound and controlled; we are going to take a closer look at you to devise strategies to contain your fire power, to neutralize your ability to damage the kingdom of darkness.*

Remember, bondage, in most cases, is a shared experience. For instance, it may be observed in a family that, across the board, marriages do not last. The reason is that most bondage often happens at the familial or ancestral level. And that is why warfare prayers at

Stage Two of the deliverance process are so critical. As you are doing warfare, you are not only affecting the individual's destiny, but you are actually affecting the destiny of the family also. It is a protracted warfare, and the devil will try to survive it. How does he do this? By trying to open your file and study what they may have on your character so that they can continue to attack your character flaws and cause you delays and frustrations.

They can do this easily because every person is born into an average family, and that family has a ruling principality detailed there by Lucifer to represent his interest in the family. And for every child that is born into that family, there is a familiar spirit detailed to monitor that child. Most often, it is that familiar spirit that trains that child in certain types of habits which the child considers his own lifestyle.

That is what Ephesians 2:1-3 is talking about. I present the exact quote here:

> **"And you hath he quickened, who were dead in trespasses and sins; Wherein in time past ye walked according to the course of this world, according to the**

prince of the power of the air, the spirit
that now worketh in the children of
disobedience: Among whom also we all
had our conversation in times past in the
lusts of our flesh, fulfilling the desires
of the flesh and the mind; and were by
nature the children of wrath, even as
others."

In the womb of sin, there were satanic powers and
demon spirits that controlled us and dictated a
program. That program was according to the plan and
purpose of the prince or power of the air, which is Satan
himself, and through such programs, he was able to
transplant certain characteristics in each one of us.
Through those characteristics, he replicated himself –
his evil nature - in each of us. When you became born-
again and liberated from the grip of the demons that
Satan has implanted in you to carry out his work, these
evil forces will try to return to attack those elements or
character traits that they had placed in you.

This is why the second stage of deliverance is very
important. As you are doing warfare, you must realize
that the Word of God is a double-edged sword. With

one edge, you are judging satanic powers that are trying to frustrate your destiny and that of your family. But it doesn't stop there; you are also pointing the other edge of that sword on to yourself. Why? You have to deal with the satanic character in you.

Suppose you are binding the devil, but you have a problem with uncontrollable anger. What happens? Every time you try to achieve something significant, the enemy simply finds a way to trigger that spirit of anger and thereby robs you of that blessing that should have come into your life. This effectively brings you back into bondage.

Aspects of our character, which have been so corrupted by the activity of the demons that lived in us before now and which have now been eliminated, must be crucified by the Word of God. When you fully yield yourself to God and those elements of the flesh are crucified, a transformation begins to take place. The nature of the enemy is broken, and the nature of God gradually replaces that. Warfare is what activates this. This is why when some persons begin to engage in warfare, the devil fights them back to throw them off track. I emphasize to people again and again: "there is no deliverance outside of the Word of God."

The Third Stage in deliverance is divine encounters for transformation. I mentioned earlier that the first stage is when you are having the demons cast out of you, and that in most cases such demons belong to the lower cadre of demons, not principalities. In the second stage, we are engaged in warfare. As you are warring, you are touching the power base of the enemy, and you are affecting the principalities.

Now, the principalities fight back by attacking your character. They have taken your entire lifetime to develop certain habits, replicating their evil nature through the demons that they put in your life, especially the work of the familiar spirit. Now, what they do, as you are growing in faith, doing warfare and increasing in anointing, they try to neutralize your faith by attacking your character weaknesses. We have to deal with this because this is where many tend to be entrapped their entire lives. Such people may have potentials and abilities, but they often do not enjoy the benefits. Why? Every time they try to make headway, the demons, having already known the character they placed in such people - whether it is lust, malice, anger, or pride - will attack their oncoming miracle and success through their character weaknesses. This is what results in the syndrome called 'failure at the edge of successes.'

WHY FAILURE AT THE EDGE OF SUCCESS?

For some people in the Body of Christ, something always seems to abort their efforts at the last minute, resulting in *failure at the edge of success*. Why at the edge of success? Because principalities can see people's seasons. And one of the most powerful strategies of the strongman is to target your seasons. When your season of lifting, promotion, and blessing is approaching, they see it, and they activate that faulty trait in your character. If you are caught, and you truly begin to misbehave, you may end up losing that season. This can lead to painful delays and fruitlessness in life and destiny.

Your seasons are your opportune times. I addressed this in greater detail in my book, *Prophetic Gateways* - where I talked about the cycles of God. There are divine cycles. There are prophetic cycles. And there is also an appointed season, which is the zone of your opportune time: the time that your gifting and your opportunities come together. It is the season for your lifting. That is the time demons love to come around you and abort your oncoming miracle.

As I already mentioned, church people are particularly prone to this syndrome. People may be very good in church. They may be committed to giving, loving, and serving. Then, suddenly, they start to misbehave. Those who are prone to gossiping start to gossip; those who are susceptible to lust start to lust; some others fall into malice, while others start to walk in pride. It is often in their season of promotion that the enemy comes to attack their character. Cheeringly, in the case of Jesus, He had a striking testimony to share: "The ruler of the world (Satan) is coming. And he has no claim on Me [no power over Me nor anything that he can use against Me]" (John 14:30, AMP). In other words, Satan could find no common ground or point of contact for him in the life of Jesus. The reason was that Jesus was fully committed to the will of God in all He did. This is the key to cutting off demonic points of contact from our lives.

I will explain more about **points of contacts** later, but for now, let's establish a few things. First, how do you overcome the strongman, the principalities, so to speak? The way to overcome them is to overcome yourself, or better put, let God overcome you.

Let me explain this with the life of Jacob. Jacob was a man who had been prone to usurpation, right from the womb. God had a prophetic destiny for him, which was profound. He had done nothing to merit this divine program; God simply chose to bless him. When he was leaving home, God met him again and reaffirmed the divine arrangement concerning his life. However, he had a nature through which the enemy could work. He, therefore, needed to be liberated from all that threatened to truncate his destiny.

Here is a summary of the stages of Jacob's deliverance. First, he was delivered from his brother who wanted to kill him. I will liken that to the first level of deliverance. In the second level of deliverance, he was with his uncle, a crafty strategist and callous taskmaster, who changed his salary ten times. Every time he tried to work against Jacob, God turned things around for his (Jacob's) good. That is the second level of deliverance – warfare. In warfare, you cannot run from the enemy; you confront him. To put it simply, in the first stage of deliverance, God delivers you *from*. In the second stage, He delivers you *in*. Hallelujah!

Interestingly, most people just want to be delivered *from*; they do not want to be delivered *in*. God did not deliver Daniel *from* the lion's den; He delivered him *in* the lion's den. You must understand that your deliverance process is intended to work out something good for you. If the devil had no purpose to fulfill in the believers' lives for our benefit, God would have taken him away completely – as it will eventually happen. But until his time is up and God takes us to heaven, we will still have to deal with him and be all the better for it.

When God delivers *from*, you are protected *from* evil. But when God delivers *in,* you are *in* the midst of the evil, you are confronting the evil, and that not only forces you to change, but also gives you authority. If God had delivered Daniel *from* the lions' den, he would not have had any authority over the lions. But by God delivering him *in* the lions' den, he confronted the lion and came out alive. The lion could not hurt him, so he came out of the lion's den as a man with authority over the lions. We can conveniently conclude that from that point in his life, the fear of lions would no longer bother him.

Jacob further underwent a third and most powerful level of deliverance, which I will discuss in the subheading below.

POWER OF DIVINE ENCOUNTERS AND TRANSFORMATION

The focus of the third level of deliverance is for God to grow our authority in the areas where we have been bruised, and firmly establish us in dominion and bring about total transformation in our lives. This is to ensure that the enemy completely loses his power over our lives. In the case of Jacob, we have seen how he was delivered *from* Esau, and later delivered *in* the house of Laban; but by the time God met him after he had left Laban, something happened to him.

That account is recorded in Genesis 32:24-30. The Bible says Jacob wrestled with "a man" (an angel) all night, and the man touched him. This supernatural man was actually the Lord Jesus in His spirit nature. He touched the hollow of Jacob's thigh and it went out of joint. So, technically, God disabled Jacob. Why? Because his seeming ability was his problem. He believed so much in his natural slyness, which made him to always do things on his own terms. And, as long as he continued to approach life this way, the enemy could easily program, predict, and contain him.

This is why many people, including believers, have issues. We do things in our own strength, not knowing that the enemy already has his program within us. If we do not allow God to have his way in our lives, the enemy can always predict and contain us by aborting our seasons. But the moment we accept transformation, which is the purpose of deliverance, we will outsmart the enemy. Why would God want to deliver us and bless us with material things if we would still continue to be like the devil and end up in hell? Evidently, therefore, the whole focus of deliverance is for us to become like God.

Still, on Jacob, the Bible says that as the heavenly being touched him, the hollow of his thigh went out of joint, and Jacob realized he was dealing with God. He consequently surrendered and asked to be blessed. God granted his request and told him that he would no longer be called Jacob but Israel. He was thus transformed from a cheat, liar, and con artist to become a prince of God. In other words, the nature of the demon that was placed in him was cleaned out and replaced by the nature of Christ.

The Bible further says that having been so transformed, Jacob "had power with God and with man", and thus prevailed. God disabled him so he was compelled to depend on God. God who disabled him would have to fight for him. When we lose our strength, we will lose our fight to God; and then, God takes over our fight. Without spiritual brokenness, we can never subdue the demonic prince that controls our family. That wicked power will continue to reproduce our forefathers' experiences in our lives. It is a generational thing.

We often have to deal with generational issues, but you cannot overcome generational issues by just praying. You also have to overcome generational characteristics that the ancestral spirit controlling the family has dictated from generation to generation. As we overcome that, our nature will become transformed into the image of Christ, and the hold of the evil one will be broken.

The Bible says that when Jacob left Peniel, where he had met with God, he said, "I have seen God face to face, and my life is preserved" (verse 30). He was simply saying that he had gone through the gates of death, and now possessed a resurrected life. The devils cannot handle a resurrected life.

We are also told that the sun rose as Jacob departed. The sun rose upon Jacob. The Sun of Righteousness wants to rise upon us. If we wholeheartedly allow this process to happen, the spotlight of God's blessing and promotion will be upon us, and we will acquire spiritual authority to help others. This is the direction of authentic deliverance.

BREAKTHROUGH PROPHETIC DELIVERANCE PRAYERS

1. Everlasting Father, you abound in mercies, longsuffering, forgiving iniquities and sins to a thousand generations of them that love and obey you. Today, I declare my everlasting love for you and your word. I ask your pardon for the occult involvement of my ancestors and the sin of rebellion against your will and order.

2. I invite the blood of the Everlasting Covenant (Hebrews13.20) to invade the foundations / generations of my family and erase all occult signs, marks, webs and destroy all forms of occult bondage from every member of my family.

3. Today, every inherit occult abilities corrupting and counterfeiting the glorious gift of God in my / our lives, catch fire and be reduced to ashes in the Mighty Name of Jesus.

4. Lord teach me how to correctly interact with your glorious Holy Spirit and grant me discernment on how to identify lying, seducing and counterfeit spirits. Keep me from error of the wicked in the mighty name of Jesus.

5. Lord God, I fully embrace your total deliverance in my life. Help me to stand strong in your love, unshaken by satanic distractions and external manipulations.

6. I take authority over the power of failure at the edge of success. Let the strategy of this spirit be exposed and destroyed in Jesus Name.

More Reasons for Delay in Deliverance Cases

1. NEED FOR A BIGGER VISION

I thank God for the deliverance and warfare transformation taking place in the Church today. Sadly, however, we are mostly reducing these happenings to the physical manifestations – with little or no emphasis on character building. Without character building, we cannot handle our inheritance in God. Of course, we can have miracles but can we handle our inheritance?

There is a vast difference between seeking after miracles and understanding our proper roles in destiny and then developing the mental capacity to embrace the bigger picture. Miracles, as good as they may seem, are merely God's way of responding to our crises through time; but His original design is to develop our moral stamina and build our mental capacity to function in our inheritance as heirs of God and joint-heirs with Christ.

It is time for the much needed mental shift from a mere preoccupation with miracles of survival to building an army of believers who can wield spiritual authority and break the curse over their families, communities, cities and nations. To walk in true power, we need to reposition the Church from being a place for seeking the blessing to a place where one becomes the curse-breaker of the generation.

God's people must be trained to embrace and exercise our inheritance; otherwise, we cannot be significantly used of God, and neither can we handle the devil effectively.

"Yet, without character building we cannot handle our inheritance in God. Of course we can have miracles but can we handle our inheritance?"

Without this crucial reorientation, Satan will continue to seek to tamper with our firepower. We would be like the children of Israel whom Pharaoh told, *You can go, but only the men, the women, and children. Leave your flock and herd behind. Leave your stuff behind. Do not go very far* (Exodus 10:24). This is much like serving God on conditions dictated by the evil one, and we must never allow this.

Moses and the children refused to yield to Pharaoh in Egypt; we also must boldly refuse to be compromised by the enemy. Thank God for Moses. He simply replied Pharaoh, *No, we will go with our wives; we will go with our children; we will go with our stuff; in fact, we are going with some of your stuff.* Eventually, the Israelites demanded of the Egyptians silver and gold and spoiled them.

Indeed, God is waiting for deliverers who will go all the way, so that He can entrust them with the inheritance and the riches of the world; so that they can do a great work for Him. You are one of those God wants to use. This is why you must take up the revelations and principles in this book and use them to take your inheritance. You must become that next great person in your family, in your nation, in your generation, and in the Church of Jesus Christ.

2. DEALING WITH POINTS OF CONTACT

Points of contact, in deliverance, are the loopholes that the enemy has established to reinforce or exert his authority over our lives. They constitute the legal grounds for him to keep meddling with our lives. Satan often manages to establish some legal basis in people's lives (in their time of ignorance) from where he can continue to maintain his evil relevance. We have to identify these points of contacts and dislodge them.

When Israel as a nation was going into the land of promise, God warned them about the issue of points of contact. He particularly warned them about the high places of the land of Canaan. The high places were hills where the Canaanite tribes served their false gods, and God knew that the tendency was there for the children of Israel to go up there, renovate those same places, and begin to defile themselves therein (which, in fact, they eventually did). Thus, God emphatically told them:

> **"Ye shall utterly destroy all the places, wherein the nations which ye shall possess served their gods, upon the high mountains, and upon the hills, and under every green tree: And ye shall overthrow their altars, and break their pillars, and burn their groves with fire; and ye shall hew down the graven images of their gods, and destroy the names of them out of that place"** (Deuteronomy 12:2-3).

CATEGORIES OF POINTS
OF CONTACT

A. CURSED ITEMS

These are items that have been dedicated to the devil. They include items that were originally inspired by the enemy and then produced and released into the market. Most people who travel to different cultures have indiscriminately bought things in those cultures that they thought were mere works of art (items from occult temples, for instance) and brought them home – not realizing the spiritual implications. Some buy crafts and other works of art from places like Africa and Asia but do not realize that some of these artifacts are carved faces of demons or replicas of demonic idols. These collectors often consider such items beautiful but, alas, they are cursed items; and thus they invite demonic presence into their lives.

It was for this reason that when the Israelites were to pass through Jericho to enter into the land of Canaan, God told them not to touch anything in the city because the place was wholly given to idolatry and everything in it was polluted. Unfortunately, a devious and greedy man, named Achan, saw a beautiful Babylonian garment and a wedge of gold and took those things into

119

his own home, bringing a curse upon the entire nation (Joshua 7).

Any item dedicated to the worship of idols or inspired by Satan - books, videotapes, cartoons or any similar thing - will invite the presence of the demons when you bring them into your home. And so, to get rid of those demons, you have to identify what those things are, and remove them from your home.

B.   DEMONIC SYMBOLISMS

There are people, for instance, who have certain types of dreams, and once they have such dreams, they will experience certain types of occurrences. Such dreams become a point of contact. Why? The devil's vocabulary has been built into these people's belief system through such dreams from which they get the message as to what to expect when they have such dreams.

There are some people that at certain times when their hand is itching, they believe that this means they will receive monetary gifts, but this is occult-based thinking. It is a point of contact. Even though you may indeed get the money, it is the devil fulfilling his purpose of binding you in a much stronger way. There is no such thing as an itchy hand bringing money in the Bible. Anything that is not from the Word of God is a ground for satanic oppression and bondage.

Again, there are some who believe that if they feel a particular way in a certain part of their body, they will experience a misfortune. Unknown to them, this is actually a satanic code, which is a point of contact. I call it a satanic code because he has programmed such people to believe that system of control. It is the negative law of faith because when you see such things, you expect certain reactions, and your expectation gives the power or authorization to the enemy to fulfill them.

This is why you must learn to live by the Word of God only. If you used to have a pattern of these types of experiences before you came to Christ, now that you are in Christ, you must go through counseling, meet with your pastor, renounce the satanic belief system, believe the Word of God, and consciously think and act contrary to the expectations of Satan. The enemy's power will be broken over your life.

C. DUMB IDOLS OR DEMON SPIRITS

I will take the Word of God on this directly. **"Now concerning spiritual gifts, brethren, I would not have you ignorant. Ye know that ye were Gentiles, carried away unto these dumb idols, even as ye were led"** (1 Corinthians 12:1-2).

The Corinthians, before they came to Christ, had been possessed by Satan through dumb idols or demon spirits. Those demon spirits led them down a certain path that built certain character traits into their nature. I referenced this earlier when I was talking about the final stage in deliverance and the need for character transformation.

If there is a Luciferian spirit functioning in a family, members and descendants of such a family will be mostly arrogant and unteachable. That character trait is not of God, it is demonic, and the demons will use it even after an individual has come to Christ.

There are Abbadon spirits that bind certain families to immorality. The members wallow and revel in it. The Corinthian church provides a good case study here. Even though they had the nine gifts of the Spirit in operation, yet they would be drunk in Holy

Communion services, and one of them could even be boasting of sleeping with his father's wife in the church – a supposedly born-again Christian!

Paul observed that the Corinthian city was bound by the Abaddon spirit (spirit of destruction). Abaddon, the principality in charge of immorality, had so much influence on the city that people would come to do business and then go to the temple where there were free women. This demonic lifestyle of free immoral sexual activity that had previously bound the believers in Corinth in their past life was carried into their Christian experience. This was why Paul had to address them severally on the issue of sexual immorality.

Now, apply this to yourself. What is there in your past life that is trying to transfer into your Christian experience? There are some people, mostly Africans, who used to go to traditional occult sources to look for visions. Usually, when people like that come to Christ, they are often looking for prophets to help them solve whatever challenges that confront them.

Don't get me wrong. There are genuine prophets. They can come to you during a prophetic meeting, and you get a word from the Lord, which is good. But when you start looking for prophets to prophesy to you before you can make decisions in your life, there is a serious problem somewhere. And it is this loophole that the devil will exploit to send some false prophets to bring confusion and crisis to your life.

If you want prophecy, open your Bible. That is the prophecy that can never fail. I am not saying this to despise prophesying or the office of prophets. I am saying this to emphasize that the prophetic ministry is one thing that has been so severely abused by the principality called Leviathan. He is corrupting it, and whole generations of people in the church are practicing witchcraft and self-hypnosis, not knowing that they are in occult bondage.

What I am saying here is this: certain habits that we acquired when we were without God were habits that the enemy wanted us to exhibit for life. He programmed them himself because they are part of his nature. If we do not deal with these habits, they become points of contact for recycled bondage. If you have anger, deal with it. The Bible says, **"Be ye angry, and sin not: let not the sun go down upon your wrath:**

Neither give place to the devil" (Ephesians 4:26-27).

One of the hallmarks of witchcraft is malice and unforgiveness. People think that you can only be called a witch if you

> *"One of the things that witchcraft spirits do is that they maintain hurts in our minds."*

regularly go to the coven and eat human flesh. This is a myopic perception of witchcraft. There are witches in the church who never go to the coven. These are people who never forgive anybody. There are husbands who are witches without realizing it. They never forgive and never forget. What your wife did ten years ago is fresh in your memory, and you remember it as if it happened yesterday. That's witchcraft – un-forgiveness. It is there. It is latched into your system, and the devil uses it to hold you back from your destiny.

What does the Bible say about forgiveness? **"Be kind one to another, tenderhearted, forgiving one another, even as God for Christ sake has forgiven you"(Ephesians 4:32)**. If you are a believer who cannot forgive, it means you are hard-hearted. And since there can't be a hard-hearted believer, it means you are practicing witchcraft. You only go to church for show, and you don't even know it. This means that, apart from witchcraft, you also have the problem of ignorance. And where does ignorance lead? Destruction! God says, **"My people are destroyed for lack of knowledge..." (Hosea 4:6)**.

We cannot lie against the truth and pretend to be Christians. Tenderheartedness is a hallmark of Christianity. One of the things that witchcraft spirits do is that they maintain hurts in our minds. What was done to you years ago, they maintain a fresh hurt there. Why? They use your wound to keep you bound to your past, so you are not advancing. This is why we must learn to let go and let God heal us. When we are healed and made whole, the enemy can no longer use us.

3. JEWELRY, LITERATURE, VIDEO MATERIALS, AND MUSIC THAT ARE DEDICATED TO SATAN

Satan places curses upon anything dedicated to him. And when you place such, whether on your body, or in your car or your home, demonic presence will be invoked. You must do away with such things so that your deliverance will not be delayed.

God wants His people to be separated from anything that defiles either our spirit or body. We must allow the Word of God to do a complete work in our lives. We are to take authority and control our dwelling places. Your children would want to access occult-projecting channels or programs on your TV, and this could bring the whole house under occult oppression and bondage. This is why there is constant tension in some houses. The atmosphere is toxic. But go to other houses where people pray all the time, and you would find the atmosphere is so peaceful and inviting.

4. HIDDEN CURSES

Delay in deliverance could result from unidentified curses and covenants in the family which have not been broken. These types of curses will perpetuate problems in people's lives. For instance, during the conquest of Jericho, Joshua, the servant of God declared that whoever attempted to rebuild Jericho would set up the foundation with the death of his firstborn and he would set up the gates with the death of his last born. About 500 years down the line, a man by the name of Hiel the Bethelite, not knowing this curse, came and started rebuilding Jericho. As he laid the foundation of the city, his firstborn died, and while setting up the gates, his last born died (1 Kings 16:34). That was an example of a hidden existing curse which was still effective over 500 years later.

There are other types of hidden curses which may not be of long duration. Sometimes curses can come from the way we relate to persons of authority. If for instance, you do not relate well with your pastor, employer, or with your parents, you can incur curses. These hidden curses can hurt you. There are people who are in churches but do not understand these things. They trivialize the anointing of their pastor while honoring visiting ministers. Such people can incur curses on themselves.

In the home, the husband occupies the office of a husband, while the wife has her place. If couples do not relate properly, they can violate moral territorial laws and incur curses. In fact, I am finding out that one of the strongest areas where witchcraft powers are effective in checking the progress of families is in marriage. A marriage may be romantic, yet spiritually bankrupt. If you do not reverence your husband by Bible standards, you will violate things in the spirit realm. If the man does not nurture and show understanding and consideration for the wife according to Bible standards, he will rupture things in the spirit and open the family in spiritual nakedness to the devil. More on this in my book, *War Is Normal*.

One of the effective ways by which the enemy builds different points of contact is to set up unidentified altars in our lives. Altars can be built around habits and appetites that do not honor God. These violate the presence of God in the family. The enemy could work with such loopholes to checkmate the progress of the family for years. People can be in the same spot for years. Why? Because the enemy has set up altars of anger, insubordination, rebellion, gluttony and other obsessive behaviors that have not been submitted to God for cleansing. These will serve to impede the progress of the family.

So, if you want your deliverance to be quick and successful, you have to obviously identify those points of contact that the enemy uses in recycling bondage and perpetuating his presence and control over your life.

BREAKTHROUGH PROPHETIC DELIVERANCE PRAYERS

1. Lord, increase my mental capacity to fill the role you have assigned to my life and destiny. Increase my vision of all that I can be and do.

2. I come against every demonic point of contact in my beliefs, life, and around my dwelling in the Name of Jesus. Be located by fire and burn in Jesus Name.

3. Holy Spirit of the living God; reveal any cursed items or objects in my life and home in the Name of Jesus.

4. God of fire, locate by your Spirit, sources of hidden curses and personal attitudes promoting and reinforcing these patterns in my life and help me uproot them once and for all in the mighty Name of Jesus Christ.

6

Other Reasons for Delay in Deliverance Cases

HIDDEN ALTARS

An altar is a spiritual point of exchange. Under the Old Covenant, God told His people to consecrate hallowed places to serve as altars whereby His people could bring Him sacrifices. Those sacrifices represented points of submission and consecration to do and to live in the will of God. They were binding places of blessings. God would meet with His people at the altar, commune with them, and transmit His blessings to them while receiving their worship.

The enemy seeks to maintain an illegal hold over people by creating certain types of altars. There are, in some families, existing altars that are generational in nature. That is to say, the ancestors of a family could have raised up altars where they served and worshiped the devil.

And even though those altars are no longer there in the physical, they are still there in the spiritual realm. Even after the next generations have come and moved on to modern family life, with some becoming Christians, the altars remain intact. They can only be demolished in spiritual warfare. This is why some unexplainable dream encounters happen where a born-again Christian finds himself in some bizarre situations in the dream life.

I remember when, some years ago, I was ministering in Europe and I ran into a wonderful servant of God. The Lord told me that he had a sentence of death upon him and I wanted to know more. The Lord told me that his lineage served as a priesthood to the devil but that that generation had gone. However, being in the line of the male generation, he was supposed to have continued the priesthood, but he came to know the Lord. He dedicated his life to the Lord and completely renounced the devil; but the Lord said to me: "Even though He is serving Me, he is represented on the altar of the enemy."

So, to break that power, the Lord gave me a prescription which was quite uncommon. The man was to be adopted by another servant of God who had a higher authority. This way, God no longer considers his genealogy after his fleshly heritage. There is some precedence of this in the Bible. In the case of

> *"Demonic altars lead to barrenness of the spirit – having potentials without success."*

Joseph, for instance, the children he had in Egypt before Jacob arrived were taken up by Jacob and placed directly under his own genealogy. They were reckoned like other sons of Jacob. So, Joseph as a father became like a brother to his own children.

There are other types of demonic altars that Satan actively seeks to erect in the lives of the children of God. These could be in the form of habits – habits that people do not repent of, such as anger, lust, gluttony, pornography, etc. In the Book of Acts, the Bible talks about the Athenians having different types of altars to different gods and Paul said they even had an altar to the 'unknown god.' Our negative habits that we do not repent of can constitute a demonic altar – an altar to an unknown god that the devil can work through to attract our worship, neutralize our effectiveness, and abort our seasons. This can cause painful delays.

As a matter of fact, when I was studying about ancestral spirits, I found out that what they often do is to replicate the nature of the familiar spirit in the character of an individual. When the person begins to advance in the things of God, they repeatedly come visiting with the negative character trait that can hold him to a lifetime of bondage.

Altars of the enemy cause delay because once the enemy can repeatedly predict and abort our prophetic cycles and seasons of blessings, they can be aborted over and over again. It is as a woman who has been pregnant nine times and suffering miscarriage on each occasion. It means that over the course of those nine pregnancies, she had no baby to show for her efforts. Demonic altars lead to the barrenness of the spirit - having potentials without results.

This is why I often say deliverance must be taught through the Word of God so that people can understand those aspects of their character that are under demonic manipulations. This knowledge will help them to crucify and yield all aspects of their character to God. Thus, the profaned ground in the human soul and personality will be sanctified, hallowed, and reclaimed, and the power of the controlling spirit will be broken.

The Prey of the Terrible

> "Shall the prey be taken from the mighty or the lawful captive delivered? But thus saith the Lord, Even the captives of the mighty shall be taken away, and the prey of the terrible shall be delivered: for I will contend with him that contendeth with thee, and I will save thy children" (Isaiah 49:24-25).

What does 'the prey of the terrible' mean? It means that the spiritual power that is binding the individual is at such a severe level. This could be either because of the high level of authority of that demonic power- the enemy's power relative to the individual's helpless state, or because the bondage has been of a very long duration, and thus the enemy has successfully established a basis and system of control. It is rightly called 'the prey of the terrible' because it looks like this is a hopeless case; nothing can be done to salvage the prey. It is like trying to take a rat from the teeth of a hungry lion.

THE LAWFUL CAPTIVE

The Lawful Captive involves someone who has himself violated spiritual territory and is therefore legitimately, as it were, bound by the satanic power. Cheeringly, God's promise is that "Even the captives of the mighty shall be taken away, and the prey of the terrible shall be delivered: for I will contend...." This assures us that with God, there are no impossible cases.

There is also something we must consider here - the contending power of the Lord. Let me give you two examples of this in the ministry of the Lord Jesus Christ.

One day, Jesus was coming down from the mountain when He saw people gathered around His disciples. He queried why they were questioning His disciples. Someone spoke up – the father of a young man who had been bound by a demon. He said, "Master, I have brought unto thee, my son, which hath a dumb spirit; And wheresoever he taketh him, he teareth him: and he foameth, and gnasheth with his teeth, and pineth away: and I spake to thy disciples that they should cast him out, and they could not." Jesus said to him, "If thou canst believe, all things are possible to him that believeth." And the man said, "Lord, I believe; help thou mine unbelief."

At that point, the demons went into action and tried to distract Jesus, but Jesus was not about to be drawn into battle with the enemy. He does not fight on the enemy's terms or invitation. So, He asked the Father, "For how long has he been this way?" The father said, "From since he was a child. Often, it tries to throw him into the water, into the fire; it seeks to destroy him." Jesus rebuked the demon, and it left the child, and he looked like he was dead. Jesus took him by the hand and delivered him to the father (Mark 9:14-27).

This was a very severe case that required a certain level of authority to break. When cases like these are brought to the church, if the required authority is not there, the case will be prolonged. The disciples of Jesus later asked him, "Why could not we cast him out?" He said to them, "This kind can come forth by nothing, but by prayer and fasting." So we know that there are some cases that can be called "this kind…"

What is the role of prayer and fasting? To unearth the secrets. Also, Jesus queried to find out the nature and extent of demonic possession. He learned that the affliction had been there from childhood. That is a strongman demon there. Another way to know is straight from the Holy Spirit through discernment. Jesus discerned what was in operation, its duration, and all the relevant information. One of the reasons we encourage pre-deliverance sessions, fasting, and waiting on the Lord is to gather specific information that is relevant to the case so that it can be handled better. That information will release a level of authority that will break the resistance of the enemy.

The unfortunate thing is that, most often, we do not take the time to prepare. We just do haphazard work, and the oppressed continue to endure their pain. This fasting and prayer and pre-ministry intercession will be helpful in dislodging these types of cases.

Another example is that of the demoniac of Gadara (Mark 5). This man was in the tombs, crying day and night, cutting himself. He had often been bound with chains to restrain him, but he was so demonically possessed that he plucked the chains asunder. However, when Jesus came by, he fell down and worshiped Him. His soul obviously yearned for God, but the bondage was much. We know it was much because Jesus rebuked the unclean spirit, the demon that was in the spirit of the man. That was the spirit seeking sexual pleasure through cutting, which the man was practicing. However, that demon initially boasted, "My name is Legion, for we are many."

One legion is over 6000 soldiers, according to the Roman army. So the demons were over 6000. It is no wonder that when Jesus cast the demons out, and they ran into a herd of swine, the swine couldn't cope. They all ran into the river. So, here, we see another case. The Bible says that after Christ's intervention, the man who had been so mad, who had been so terrible, was cured instantly and came to his right mind.

I must emphasize that the degree of authority that Jesus exhibited here is at the glory level. There are levels of authority. There is an anointing of power, but there is also the glory level of anointing. At the glory level, the flesh is totally extinct. It is God and the devil. And, of course, when the glory of

"The unfortunate thing is that, most times, we do not take time to prepare. We just do haphazard work and the oppressed continue to endure their pain."

God collides with evil, evil bows instantly.

I remember in 1986; we were ministering deliverance to a wonderful young woman. I was in fact initially doing the deliverance from 7 p.m. to 10 p.m. and wasn't making any headway. One of the anointed vessels, a lady came by, uninvited, to help us. Immediately she arrived, the demons recognized her authority and were attempting to attack her. She commanded them to bow, and they bowed, and we began casting them out. After about 300 demons had left the sister, we had still not gone anywhere. I was tired, burnt out; so, I laid on my back.

Then, I had a vision. I saw a mountain that was full of darkness. In the middle of it, a flickering light began. That light grew stronger and stronger until it became brighter than the brightness of the noonday. Instantly, my hands were flung in the air as I exclaimed, "the glory of the Lord, the glory of the Lord, the glory of the Lord!" The atmosphere of the room changed. The demon-oppressed lady, under the active manifestation of the demon, looked terrified. She looked around and started screaming; the demons ran out of her instantly. When the glory of God shows up, it is a very wonderful thing to behold.

Demonic Cycles

There are demonic cycles, just as you have the cycles of God – comprising spiritual cycles, prophetic cycles, and appointed seasons (this you can read about in my book, *Prophetic Gateways*). Demonic cycles are cycles within which certain demons execute their evil programs in the life of an individual, a family or a nation.

At certain times in the course of the year, some people are sick. In some families, when people reach a particular age, they must suffer reverses. Some individuals, within specific months, in the course of the year, must suffer unexplainable, unaccountable reverses. Perhaps any of these illustrations relates to your personal life. What you need to do is to consecrate yourself to break the power of the demons that are behind the reverses, misfortunes, and afflictions in your life. You can actually mobilize other people, or other members of your family and target the base of those demonic powers, break them asunder, and force out a release of God's program in your life.

Understanding demonic cycles in your life are vital. The Holy Spirit will point this out to you because He will monitor you and will let you see the trend over time and know what to do.

Now, there are some cases that are so surreal that even the minister who is doing the deliverance has to apply wisdom because there is so much that the human nature or personality can take. Many years ago, I was ministering to a young woman. I do not know what happened to her when she was young, but it had so severely altered her personality that as we were ministering deliverance on her, tons of demons were eliminated; but we got to the point where we felt that inner restraint to stop because she could not take it anymore. If we had put in more pressure, it would have led to a breakdown, and that would have been counterproductive.

So, we had to stop and ask the Holy Spirit to take charge of her. We laid hands on her, blessed her, and ministered healing. There were some intricate healings that needed to be worked at the soul level, and the Holy Spirit knew exactly what to do.

That is why, again, I will say, anointing is good, but skill is needed to go with the anointing. You develop skill by being called to pay special attention to a particular area of ministry, and through continuous practice in that area, skill is developed. Consequently, with anointing and skill, you can more appropriately respond to the Holy Spirit's strategy for achieving results.

One of the things that cause a delay in deliverance, which I mentioned previously under lawful captivity, is that there are people who want God and the devil at the same time. People

> *"People professing faith in God go about sleeping around and engaging in other forms of depravity that validate the enemy's presence in their lives."*

want to give God a wedding suit and the devil a wedding gown and combine the best of both worlds. It does not work that way. The Bible says God cannot be tempted with evil, neither does He tempt any man with evil. If any man is tempted, he is being drawn away by his lust. This means we have to deal with our lusts. We cannot have one leg in the world and one leg in the Kingdom and expect things to work.

It's so painful to observe that much of modern-day practice of Christianity is a perversion by the wicked one. We are constantly being told about the God of love but not the God who calls us to accountability. People professing faith in God go about sleeping around and engaging in other forms of depravity that validate the enemy's presence in their lives. The Bible says that **"Whosoever is born of God doth not commit sin; for his seed remaineth in him: and he cannot sin because he is born of God" (1 John 3:9)**. It also says **such a person keeps himself and the evil one is not able to touch him (1 John 5:18)**. If you keep yourself in the love of God, then the enemy will not be able to bind or to touch you.

Illegal Collections

Another thing that can cause delay is ignorance. Ignorance can permit the enemy to perpetuate what I call illegal collections. Demonic spirits are like debt collectors. They claim that there are covenants or curses in place and so they move in to collect their "dues" by visiting the individual with affliction, sickness, reverses, struggle, oppression, suppression, depression, pain, and retrogression. However, the Word of God counters this deception of the enemy. The Bible says that every handwriting of ordinances that was against us or stood hostile and contrary to us, He

Himself, the Lord Jesus, took it out of the way, blotted it out by His own blood, and nailed it to the Cross (Colossians 2:14).

So, if every negative handwriting, obligation or contract has been blotted out by the Blood of Christ, how come the enemy is still collecting on people? Through ignorance. Ignorance of the law limits your ability to enforce your rights. When you know what belongs to you, what your rights are, you can go to the devil, with that written Word of God and confront him.

Again, I must say that knowledge of the truth is not enough. Our faith is not a passive faith; it is an active, warring faith. In case you do not know, you are supposed to be fighting – fighting the good fight of faith. If you merely quote Scriptures while the enemy is fighting you, how will you be able to take advantage of your spiritual authority and break his aggression? We are to fight meaningfully and purposefully. That way, we can destroy the enemy's delay in our lives.

Ancestral Spirits

Finally, to sum it up, I will go again to the subject of ancestral spirits. I mentioned this when I began to talk about the congregation of the dead. What do I mean by ancestral spirit? I mean the controlling power of your family.

Let me use the African culture for instance. In African culture or cosmological composition, the family has two dimensions – the natural, physical dimension, and then the spiritual dimension. The natural dimension of the family is composed of father, mother, and the children; whereas in the spiritual dimension of the family, according to African cosmological orientation, the family also includes the ancestors or the fathers who have passed on. These dead entities are regarded as representing the family on the spiritual plane and having a valid contribution to make to the day-to-day well being of the physical or natural family.

For this reason, therefore, a number of sacrifices are done in certain seasons of the year to appeal for the continued support, guidance, and help of the ancestors. The truth of the matter is that this is just a satanic philosophy because the Bible says **it is appointed unto man once to die and after that the judgment (Hebrews 9:27).**

Once a person is dead, they no longer have any influence on the living. They have no power or control of any kind. Instead, they immediately face divine judgment – the outcome of which will depend on whether they lived for God (which will make them to be received by Him), or whether they lived for the devil (which makes them liable to a retribution consequent to their poor choices.) Either way, the point is that they no longer have any relevance on the living.

So, who fills the gap? Who comes through dreams to manifest as the departed one? It is that ancestral spirit, Satan's delegate that has controlled the family for generations, masquerading as their late forefathers, drawing worship from the family and assigning punishment to every member of the family.

The first level in Satan's use of ancestral spirits is to attach a familiar spirit to everyone born into a family. This familiar spirit is used to train a child and put habits in that child that will enable the Luciferian program for the family to be extended and manifested in the life of that child. This is how a familiar spirit busies itself as the child grows up, putting different types of habits into him. These habits gradually form a part of the individual's character, and he soon begins to think, *this is my life; I am living my life.* Sadly, he is not living his life; he is living according to the dictates of the devil through the ancestral spirit.

The Bible talks about the prince of the power of the air, the spirit that now works in the children of disobedience (Ephesians 2:2). This spirit that works in the children of disobedience seduces and implements the program of Lucifer for each member of a family. When someone born into such family eventually comes to Christ, he wants to enjoy the benefits of his relationship with Christ; he wants to exhibit spiritual power and authority – but what happens? The ancestral spirits simply call for his file according to the habits in which they had been grooming him over the years, and they begin to attack him through his character. If it is anger they had put in him, they nurture this anger and begin to work with that. Or it could be some other forms of lusts, perversions, and addictions with which they choose to work. They begin to stir up those base instincts, using them to attack and abort his seasons. This is the greatest source of delay for a believer.

There is a power called the spirit of delay. It is Satan's most powerful weapon in ensuring that people are non-achievers in life. It delays and then aborts. Understanding your history, family line, and structure will give you the revelation and momentum you need to conquer this spirit.

I remember a wonderful sister I once ministered to in the course of my pastoral work years ago. When she came to see me, she was 36 years old at the time. She said, "Pastor, Please, I am 36 years old, I have been a faithful Christian and a virgin. For all these years, no man has ever proposed to me, not even to give me the opportunity to say no. What is wrong?" I said, "I do not know, but we can pray."

The Bible says **if the foundation is destroyed what can the righteous do? (Psalm 11:3).** Well, the righteous can pray and rebuild the foundation. So I set for her three days of fasting and prayers so that we could pray together. On the first day of the fast, I brought myself to the Lord and was presenting her case before the Lord. Suddenly, I drifted away in the spirit, and I saw four huge, menacing, ferocious dogs walking towards me and asking me in a human voice, "Is it by power? Is it by power?" trying to knock me down. And I replied, "It is not by power, nor by might but by my spirit, says the Lord. I come against you by the power of the Living God."

I opened my eyes and asked God what the revelation meant. God told me those were the Abaddon spirits in charge of her family and that they were the ones that had held her in captivity. On the third day, the sister and I got together to pray. Other prophetic things came up belonging to another chapter of another book.

Suffice it to say that these powers can cause really heartbreaking delays. To break their stronghold, you have to know your family history and what incriminating traits are in your character. Otherwise, a man of God can labor, fast and pray, and nothing happens. You may even get some release, but that power can come back to attack your next season. His ability to attack your season is based on the character traits he has placed in you.

This is why you must identify the loopholes in your character and bring them into submission to the Word of God. Once the Word of God works on you, that area of your life is broken and cleaned out. From that point, the evil power will lose its hold on you, and you can then proceed to live a productive, fruitful life, to the glory of God.

BREAKTHROUGH PROPHETIC DELIVERANCE PRAYERS

1. Every hidden altar channeling evil into my life and family; catch fire and be destroyed in the name of Jesus.

2. I bring any opening in my life that furnishes the enemy legal rights against me under the redeeming blood of Jesus. I declare the curse broken and nullified by the superior claims of the blood of Jesus Christ.

3. All demonic cycles of pain, reverses and struggle; be now liquidated and deactivated.

4. I decree a speedy divine arrest for all illegal demonic collectors in my life, family, and ministry. I demand and receive double restoration for everything or lost opportunities I have suffered due to illegal collection activities in the Name of Jesus.

5. The ancestral spirit delegated to monitor and undermine the glory of God in my family; you are fired in Jesus Name. Jesus is the new sheriff in town.

The Strongman of the House

"When the unclean spirit is gone out of a man, he walketh through dry places, seeking rest, and findeth none. Then he saith, I will return into my house from whence I came out; and when he comes, he findeth it empty, swept, and garnished. Then goeth he, and taketh with himself seven other spirits more wicked than himself, and they enter in and dwell there: and the last state of that man is worse than the first. Even so, shall it be also unto this wicked generation" (Matthew 12:43-45).

It is critical in deliverance to pray for discernment. Jesus clearly demonstrated what it means to have discernment. He was always very specific; and when it was necessary, He asked questions. I will reasonably assume that, if He did not ask questions, it is because it was not required for He already had insight given to Him by the Father about the particular demonic situation with which He was dealing. So, knowledge of what we are doing is necessary.

Revelation received (particularly discerning of spirits) is far more important when you have to dislodge demons from people as you move in the anointing of God. The presence and power of God may be available to deliver, but with limited knowledge and inability to benefit from the presence of the Holy Spirit at any given moment, we will run short of the kind of victory God wants us to have.

"Revelation received (particularly discerning of spirits) is far more important when you have to dislodge demons from people as you move in the anointing of God."

A remarkable encounter is recorded in Matthew 12. The Pharisees had heard about the glorious things that were being said about Jesus and His ministry, and they started castigating him out of envy and jealousy. **"But when the Pharisees heard it they said this fellow does not cast out devils but by Beelzebub, the prince of the devils" (v. 24).**

I want you to see something here. Even though we know that the Pharisees spoke out of envy, there is something significant about it. These people saw that Jesus was active in casting out devils, so they said He was doing this through the power of Beelzebub, the prince, or the chief of the devils.

Who is Beelzebub? He is, of course, the principality in charge of witchcraft - the Lord of the Flies. But what they were implying here is that Jesus had a link with the prince of the devils, so His actions were hardly surprising. If He had a relationship with the prince of the devils, then, of course, the other smaller demons would obey. The above position would apply, for instance, in the case of a false prophet who is in league with the devil and who is deceiving people. But in this particular rise, it was a malicious lie being told by the Pharisees against Jesus.

GOVERNMENTAL POWERS IN THE SPIRITUAL REALM

There is something else I want you to see in the verse above. Cadres and levels of authority exist in the realm of the spirit. This understanding is particularly important when you are doing deliverance against the strongman or the ruler of the house. Let's look at the Scriptures again to learn one or two things about this.

Jesus, in response to the accusation of the Pharisees, said, **"Every kingdom divided against itself is brought to desolation, and every city or house divided against itself shall not stand: And if I by Beelzebub cast out devils, by whom do your children cast them out? Therefore they shall be your judges. But if I cast out demons by the Spirit of God, then the kingdom of God is come unto you"** (Matthew 12:25-28).

Jesus simply told the detractors to wake up to the reality that through His demonstration of the omnipotent power of God, the Kingdom of God was in operation on the earth already. The Kingdom of God, the governmental authority of God, His presence, is here. In other words, every time demons are being dislodged and you see manifestations, it means that two kingdoms are in a clash. It implies that God's governmental authority is in action to compel obedience.

Beyond this, however, Jesus gives us a bigger clue: **How can one enter into the house of a strong man except he first binds the strong man and then spoil his goods and take his house, or dispossess him of his armor? (v. 29).** What is Jesus saying here? In many cases of demonic possession or oppression, to relieve the oppressed and dislodge the demons, you have to discern the strongman of the house and oust him. Once you overcome the strongman of the house, you will be able to liberate his captive.

Let me now refer to the house mentioned in the passage, and what is meant by the strongman. Earlier on, I noted that demons are disembodied spirits (spirits without bodies). In this same passage of Matthew 12, Jesus said something about the nature of these demon spirits. **He said when a demon is cast out of a man he goes about seeking rest but finding none. Then he says to himself, I will go back to my house, from where I came out (vv. 43-44).**

Notice that the demon said "my house." What is the demon claiming as his house? That same individual that he was occupying before. So when Jesus mentions the strongman of the house, he is referring to the gatekeeper, the doorkeeper, the one who first established his presence as the rightful owner, even though illegally, in that individual who is so oppressed or demonized.

I want you to pay proper attention to verses 44 and 45 of that passage. "**Then the demon saith, I will return into my house from whence I came out; and when he comes, he findeth it empty, swept, and garnished. Then goeth he, and taketh with himself seven other spirits more wicked than himself, and they enter in and dwell there: and the last state of that man is worse than the first Even so shall it also be unto this wicked generation.**"

Jesus is saying something far-reaching here. Who is claiming ownership of the house? One particular spirit. And when that individual spirit is cast out, he roams about and finds no rest. This means that demons are disembodied spirits and are tormented when they have no house to inhabit. That *house* is a body. During winter, it is cold out there, but you go out because you have business to do; but then, at the end of the day, you return to the warmth and comfort of your house. That aside, as humans, we tend to have some degree of psychological and emotional attachment to where we live. You are, for instance, used to the way your bathroom and kitchen are. And once there's a disruption in these settings, you get uncomfortable, and you immediately try to fix the situation.

This also applies to demons. As I said before, they do not have a body. Thus, they have to seek out a human body to occupy. And as soon as they find one, they settle themselves in there, and it becomes uncomfortable for them to leave.

To be an effective deliverance minister, when you are scheduling somebody for ministry, you need to ask the Lord, "What is the strongman?" Also, in the course of counseling, you can determine what the strongman is, that is, the predominant spirit that first got hold of the person. That is the strongman. It doesn't necessarily mean it is the strongest demon as the above Scripture shows.

In the example cited by Jesus, the demon believed that he was cast out because he was not strong enough. He thought he needed to get seven other spirits more wicked than himself to come and occupy the man. Let us look further into the Scripture, and we will see how Jesus dealt with the strongman. Here is the account in Mark 5 again:

> "And they came over unto the other side of the sea, into the country of the Gadarenes. And when he was come out of the ship, immediately there met him out of the tombs a man with an unclean spirit. Who had his dwelling among the tombs; and no man could bind him, no, not with chains: Because that he had often been bound with fetters and chains, and the chains had been plucked asunder by him, and the fetters broken in pieces: neither could any man tame him. And always, night and day, he was in the mountains, and in the tombs, crying, and cutting himself with stones" (Mark 5:1-4).

Here is something you must not overlook. What did this man have? An unclean spirit. How many is that? One. By the way, whenever the Bible talks about an unclean spirit, it has something to do with sexual perversion. Not only that, but the passage also says that no one could bind the man, which means that he was also fierce and wild indicating that this case was beyond that of an unclean spirit. There is a condition that is called masochism - which is the habit of deriving sexual pleasure from pain, including inflicting wounds on oneself. So, we know that this unclean spirit, however he gained entrance into this man, was tormenting him so badly that the man resorted to cutting himself. And I believe that with each cut, he derived some sexual pleasure, so he cut himself even more. People tried to help him, but how did they go about it? They went about it as regular religious people do. They put ropes and chains on him. But what the man needed was a real anointing. It is the anointing, not the chains, that will help a person like that.

Have you ever been to some weird places where in the name of deliverance the recipients are flogged so that the demons in them could go out? The truth, however, is that such behavior only entertains the devil. It is the anointing – not the chains or the whip – that works.

As for this demoniac, they put chains around him, and nothing worked. As a matter of fact, he broke the chains. Do you think that was natural? No. Rather, the demonic energy snapped the chains and the ropes. He moved to the mountains crying and cutting himself, seeking relief. The demons were indwelling him and sexually tormented him.

In the course of ministry in 1987, I had an encounter with a lady who had been attacked by sexual madness. I sometimes think when you see evil in its true nature, you will learn to fear God the more, be compelled to respect the Word of God, and you will appreciate the value of a relationship with God. By seeing evil in its rare manifestation, you will realize you want nothing to do with it. You will honor God the more.

Let us continue to explore this account in Mark 5.

"But when he saw Jesus afar off, he ran and worshiped him, And cried with a loud voice, and said, What have I to do with thee, Jesus, thou Son of the most

high God? I adjure thee by God that thou torment me not. For he said unto him, Come out of the man, thou unclean spirit. And he asked him, What is thy name? And he answered, saying, My name is Legion: for we are many." (vv. 6-9).

Can demons worship? Who worshiped here? The man. Even though he was carrying thousands of demons in him, when he saw his Creator, he worshiped. If you would stop for a moment and worship God with your problem, your problem will bow. The demonic bondage was heavy on this man; the real him longed for the freedom that comes from worshipping his Maker. He worshiped Jesus, and cried with a loud voice and said "What have I to do with thee, Jesus, thou Son of the highest God? I adjure thee by God that thou torment me not." Reader, please note that Jesus had already commanded the demon, saying, "Come out of the man, thou unclean spirit." Note that this was not the man responding to Jesus. It was the demon that had begun to claim his right.

In verse 9, Jesus asked the demon "what is thy name?" Why was it necessary for Jesus to ask for the name?

Observe that Jesus had just called him "thou unclean spirit;" yet he went further to ask for his specific name. It is important to note the sequence of events here. When Jesus first told the demon to come out of the man, his response was, "torment me not." He obviously didn't want to let go. Jesus knew that there was something more going on; this was why He asked for the name of the demon.

It is not in every deliverance case that we are required to ask "what is your name?" Jesus did not do that in every case. The thing is, there are no formulas in deliverance; there are simply principles. I made that mistake when I was young in deliverance work. I read books by the person whose team members delivered me, and whatever the book said to do I would do. Some of the things I followed and did to get people delivered were simply unrequired and certainly most controversial. I wanted to practice everything in the books until the Holy Spirit said, "I am the One you are to follow and not necessarily the formulas."

So, there is no formula; we just act as the Holy Spirit leads. There is no deliverance without the Holy Spirit. It is our responsibility to acknowledge Him, recognize

Him, reverence Him, respect Him, and then He will take control. Once He takes over, the yoke has to go.

When Jesus asked, "what is thy name?" the demon answered, "my name is Legion for we are many." **"And he besought him much that he would not send them away out of the country.   Now there was there nigh unto the mountains a great herd of swine feeding. And all the devils besought him, saying, Send us into the swine, that we may enter into them" (vv. 10-12).**

We already know that only one demon was speaking before. But after that demon had been addressed and the evil spirit showed reluctance, Jesus, through a release by the Holy Spirit, and also (I believe) for our learning, asked for his name. I think Jesus could have just said, "Get out!" but He wanted us to learn a principle of deliverance. Indeed, some of the miracles Jesus did were for teaching purposes.

So, the demon, in response to Jesus' question, said, "My name is Legion, for we are many."   How many constitutes a legion?   Over 6000! More than 6000 demons were living in this one person, but only one was possessing him. The others were there to back that one demon, to make sure he went nowhere. Who invited these other demons? The unclean spirit, the strongman.

Verse 12 says **"And all the devils besought him, saying, Send us into the swine, that we may enter into them."** Now, it's not just one demon that was begging Jesus; it was all of them. They begged him to send them into the swine.

I want you to know that Jesus, at this point, was functioning in one of the gifts of the Spirit called discerning of spirits. So, the veil of the spirit was torn apart, and He could see all these thousands of demons, all of them pleading for Him to send them into the swine.

The unclean spirit that originally possessed this man was represented in his character. What were his habits? He liked to stay in the tombs and the mountains. However, we know he had more than just the unclean spirit because we saw other behaviors that he exhibited such as breaking chains. An unclean spirit would not entice him to be breaking chains; he was supported by the legion. Imagine having to be bound by over 6000 demons, when one is enough to handle a human being. Even 2000 swine could not cope with the legion.

Again, we read that this man would cry and cut himself. I want us to study that because there is a correlation between medicine if it is genuine science and the spiritual things of God. There is a condition, as I mentioned before, called masochism, which is the act of deriving sexual pleasure from inflicting pain on oneself, which I think factors into this. We know it is a demonic condition, just like we know same-sex relations is a demonic condition. People just do not know. You hear them say, "Well, this is my nature." No. It is not God's original design for your life. But as soon as you accept it, then you validate it. It is a demonic condition. It is the same thing as fornication, adultery, pornography, and masturbation. All kinds of uncleanness are under this category.

I want you to understand that man is a spirit being that has a soul and lives in the body. If a man is not born-again, what part of the person is possessed? It is his spirit. Only one demon can possess the spirit and distribute his personality through the man. But the body and soul of the man can be filled up with thousands of demons, depending on how much the person can carry. Flip it on the other side. You can carry the grace of God to such a level that you wouldn't even believe it.

So, now, we have a better understanding of how to correctly handle deliverance cases as Jesus says in Matthew 12:29, **"Or else how can one enter a strong man's house, and spoil his goods, except he first binds the strong man? And then he will spoil his house."** The key is knowing the strongman. Once you dislodge him, the others have to go. Think of it this way. Once you evict the real tenant on a lease, you do not need to know the names of those on sub-leases. You just need to have the name of the person on the lease correctly.

Now, let us return to the next incident in Mark 9:14. In doing so, I must ask you, deliverance student, how do you know when you are going to encounter "this kind"? In reality, you cannot tell. So, what do you do? Live a fasted life – that is, fast and often pray and be prepared to handle challenges as they arise.

Deliverance and plenty of food cannot go comfortably together. You have to live a fasted life to be effective in deliverance ministry. You can readily preach and teach, but if you are going to move in the deliverance anointing, you needed to be fasted up and prayed up. Those two areas are critical for you to be sensitive to the Spirit. This way, you become so yielded to the Holy Spirit that instead of the demons encountering you, they are encountering the glory.

There are degrees of manifestations of power – faith, anointing, and the glory. Each is a different level. We can minister by faith without the anointing being present. We simply rebuke demons and trust that God will work. However, when the anointing is present, you move in the energy of that anointing – this is another level. But, beyond the anointing, once the glory is present, the demons leave quickly. I have had instances of this in my life and ministry. The times when we function in the anointing are excellent. But sometimes the glory comes and takes it over the top.

God is indeed awesome! I pray that we as His body will have the hunger to seek Him. Spiritual hunger is what is needed at this time. It is true that we sometimes have challenges and difficulties in our lives, but these are mere strategies of the enemy to distract and wrongly engage us. He knows that the more we are preoccupied with trying to deal with the challenges, the more spiritually naked we become. Demons know how to handle delay and hinder us once we become spiritually naked. But once the glory comes on us, corruption cannot stand, and no demonic power can stand. Let us pray that we know our Father the more, that we love Him the more, and that we get drawn into His presence even more.

Now, in looking at the case in Mark 9, please note again that Jesus never followed a formula. He did not handle this case like the other one. Why? Because He always followed the leading of the Holy Spirit. He said it clearly that **"the Son can do nothing of himself, but what he seeth the Father do..." (John 5:19)**. He was so in God and followed the Holy Spirit so much that He looked at Nicodemus and said, "Except a man is born-again..." He looked at the woman at the well, and said, "Go and call your husband." He was always on point because He followed the Holy Spirit accurately.

In this case under consideration, He was coming off the mountain

... the devil does not choose for us when to fight.

170

after having an encounter with the Father. He saw some of his disciples and a crowd was around them and the scribes were questioning them. He said, "Why are you questioning my disciples? "Then a man came forward, saying, **"Master, I have brought unto thee my son, which hath a dumb spirit; And wheresoever he taketh him, he teareth him: and he foameth, and gnasheth with his teeth, and pineth away: and I spake to thy disciples that they should cast him out; and they could not."** Jesus replied that the boy is brought to him, and as soon as the child was brought, the demon knocked him down, and he started wallowing and foaming at the mouth.

The demon was communicating something here. It was simply saying, "Okay, Jesus, we are on, let's start." But Jesus did not even look in his direction, which tells us that the devil does not choose for us when to fight. Our Commander-in-Chief, the Holy Spirit, chooses when and how we get to fight. We do not respond because we are faced with a battle and we need to react to it; if we do so, we can get sucked in. We respond only to our Head, our Master, who will then lead us in and tell us what to do.

Once the anointing of God comes upon you, there is the danger of getting distracted by manifestations. Church services are frequently disrupted this way. We can be having a deliverance conference, and before we know it, one person begins to react, and the man of God leaves the teaching, and the service becomes a circus. That is a distraction.

One time, I invited a prophet to minister, and he came with his assistant and the family of the assistant also attended. While he was ministering, the sister of the assistant began to manifest, and the prophet started to react. I turned to him and said, "No prophet, my ministers will take her to my office and go and deal with it there." The brother of the girl was so angry and openly disrespected me right in my church. I forgave him because it was ignorance.

And he came with his assistant and the family of the assistant also attended. While he was ministering, the sister of the assistant began to manifest, and the prophet started to react. I turned to him and said, "No prophet, my ministers will take her to my office and go and deal with it there." The brother of the girl was so angry and openly disrespected me right in my church. I forgave him because it was ignorance.

We did not need that prophet to cast out that devil; we had hundreds of other born-again Spirit-

We can emulate Jesus' example by deferring to the Holy Spirit

filled believers who could have simply taken that girl to my office and knocked the devil off of her, while we continued without being distracted. Jesus did not start reacting because the devil began to manifest. He seemed to be saying, "I will get to you when I am ready." What He did instead was to ask the father how long it had been since the affliction came upon the child. (Again, this was for your sake and mine). The father said it had been since childhood.

So, here, we have another instance of how a strongman is developed. There had been an opening, and the demon got in there through initiation, either by what the parents did or by what a demonic person did to the child such as molesting the child. Typically, the devil wants to get into the life of children between the ages of four and seven through molestation by close relations. It is one of the widest doors and one most frequently used. Demons can enter and will promote rejection, rape, resentment, anger, or stubbornness. All of these can enter through that initial molestation. If it happens repeatedly and undetected, when that child reaches teenage years, he or she will become promiscuous, rebellious, and impudent.

In the case of this child, Jesus clearly demonstrated discernment as usual. His primary job was to discern accurately so that the deliverance ministration would be effective. How can we emulate His example? By deferring to the Holy Spirit. By not so quickly jumping in when somebody runs to you and says they are in trouble. If you do so, you will go there and fail. It could even be a trap. The Holy Spirit is Lord! And when His Lordship is acknowledged He will produce liberty.

So, in response to the query of Jesus, the father answered, "Of a child. And ofttimes it hath cast him into the fire, and into the waters, to destroy him..." Just by that alone, Jesus got the point. And then the father added, "but if thou canst do any thing, have compassion on us, and help us." But Jesus said, "No, that is not it. It is if you can believe."

Why did Jesus say that? Why did he mention the faith of the father? If faith was necessary, which faith did He act upon when He helped the demoniac of Gadara?

Remember that when Jesus saw the Gadarene with all the demons, the man rushed forth and began to worship. By that action of worship, he was saying, "I believe you are my Creator. I am in bad condition through my fault perhaps, but you are still my Creator. I worship you." In this case of this father, it was a different thing entirely. This father apparently had gone to different places. We do not know what he had done that might have contributed to his son's condition. He did not believe his son could be healed; he only came to the disciples to try. Unfortunately, being inexperienced themselves, the disciples jumped in on trial and failed on trial. This was why Jesus became the next person for the father to try.

As soon as Jesus made the man realize that his son's healing depended on his faith, the man cried out, "Lord I believe, help thou my unbelief." That declaration was a sign of budding faith in the man. And before he could complete the sentence, Jesus had faced the demon and commanded it to depart.

This again gives me the impression that the doorway to demonic possession for the child must have come through the father. Whatever he might have done and his child took the brunt of it when he cried out like that – "Master, Adonai, I believe, help my unbelief," he opened the ground for God to step in and Jesus got ready to deal with this demon.

What do we learn from this? We have to make sure the case is ready for action. We have to prepare the case to be ready, through counseling, fasting, proper discernment, or detailed interview. Seek to reach the bottom of the situation; seek to get to the root of it by discernment or by interview so you can open the case up and get ready to kick that devil out.

> **"When Jesus saw that people came running together he rebuked the foul spirit and said unto him, Thou dumb and deaf spirit, I charge thee come out of him and enter him no more" (v.25).**

There are two things to note here. People started running. If Jesus had allowed the crowd to gather, it would have become a circus, and there would have been distractions. Christ, therefore, decided to deal with it before the environment became unmanageable. The second thing to note is that when the father spoke, he said the child had a dumb spirit – which means that he had an idea of what was wrong with the child, but his knowledge was not complete. But Jesus, seeing much deeper, said, "Thou dumb and deaf spirit…" If He had just said "thou dumb spirit," the spirit, which was also deaf would not have heard. Instead, He said "Thou dumb and deaf spirit." Jesus got the accurate discernment, and it proved very helpful to his ministration. We should pray for discernment, and if we have it, we should nurture it by practicing the presence of God, meditating on the Word of God, and staying in the presence of God.

There are places that domesticate and regulate your life into a routine. To practice the presence of God, try to move away from such places. You need to be able to come away and be quiet. Your house may not always be a good option because there are certain routines that have structured your life into a pattern. You need to go away sometimes.

Now, look at what verse 26 says – **"and the spirit came out of him and sent him and he was as one dead, and many said he is dead."** We would have thought that Jesus would speak and instantly the spirit would leave. No. The spirit tore him, renting him sore, crying. But the order had been given, and Jesus would not repeat Himself. The anointing was compelling obedience to the order Jesus had given.

A man of God said to me recently that, if you say nothing, God will confirm nothing. You have to preach His Word for Him to confirm His Word. So, if you say nothing, He will confirm nothing. What did He say? He said, "Thou deaf and dumb spirit." But we can't go everywhere saying "Thou dumb and deaf spirit" to every other spirit. In another instance (which we saw earlier), He said, "You unclean spirit come out… What is your name?" Jesus dealt specifically; Jesus dealt precisely.

Let us summarize what we have learned so far about the strongman. He is the first demon to gain access into the spirit of a person, and he can decide to host other demons who bring reinforcement. This, in a way, tells us that even the strongman knows that he has limited opportunity. Generally, demons know that one day, God, the real owner of life, is going to show up and then they will have to leave; so they prepare by reinforcing themselves.

In my country, we have a saying, "Many days for the thief, one day for the owner." Once the owner comes and catches the thief, the thief's time immediately comes to an end. Jesus is the rightful owner of life. **"For by him were all things created, that are in heaven, and that are in earth, visible and invisible, whether they be thrones, or dominions, or principalities, or powers: all things were created by him, and for him"** **(Colossians 1:16).**

I believe that some of the deliverance cases we handle fall into the category of what we call "the prey of the terrible." Isaiah 49:24–25 says:

> **"Shall the prey be taken from the mighty or the lawful captive delivered? But thus saith the LORD, Even the captives of the mighty shall be taken away, and the prey of the terrible shall be delivered: for I will contend with him that contendeth with thee, and I will save thy children.**

And I will feed them that oppress thee with their flesh; and they shall be drunken with their blood, as with sweet wine: and all flesh shall know that I the LORD am thy Saviour and thy Redeemer, the mighty One of Jacob."

Here, the mighty one of Jacob, the Lord, the Holy Spirit talks about the lawful captive and the prey of the terrible. There are lawful captives and prey of the terrible. I believe that when you look at these two high demonic cases that we have just considered, you will find the one that belongs to the lawful captive and the one that belongs to the prey of the terrible.

BREAKTHROUGH PROPHETIC DELIVERANCE PRAYERS

1. I disable the strongman and his evil strategies or enchantments to tie me down. Be exposed and expelled from my life now in Jesus' name.

2. Let the glorious light of the Living God beam upon every aspects of my life exposing the roots, tentacles and modus operands of the strongman for total divine retribution and destruction in Jesus Name.

3. Father of life, reclaim and restore every distortion and corruption of the strongman in my life in the mighty Name of Jesus Christ.

4. God of glory touch and heal me. The God of Wonders, where I have been damaged the most, release a higher level of authority in and through to bring healing to others in the Mighty Name of Jesus Christ.

OVERCOMING DELAY FACTORS IN DELIVERANCE

Seven Urgent Messages to the Churches

Some time ago, the Lord called my attention and gave me these seven points to deliver to His Body, the Church. According to what the Lord said, if these seven things are not handled carefully, then the charismatic Pentecostal church will become like semi-occult churches. So, we are to pay attention to these, so that the devil, our enemy, will not be able to destroy the Church from within.

Jesus Christ Is the Message of the Entire Bible

From Genesis to Revelation, God the Father, through God the Holy Spirit, is presenting revelations of His Son. The Lord Jesus Christ is who God wants to reveal. He wants us to see His Son who He loves so much and is willing to deliver up for our sins. Whatever topics we preach - whether salvation, prosperity, deliverance, healing or breakthrough - we must reckon with the fact that the revelation of Jesus Christ is the message of gospel.

If Jesus Christ had not come in the flesh to be born, suffer, die and be raised again from the dead, there would have been no message to preach, no ministry, no church, no minister. The Person of the Lord needs to feature prominently in our messages and songs. God wants the whole world to know His magnificent Son. This is the burden of the Almighty! How desperately today's Church need to return to that simplicity of the gospel and present Jesus Christ and Him crucified.

Redemption Is By the Blood

The foundation of true Christianity is the testimony of Blood of the Son of God. He is the Lamb slain from the foundation of the world. We are not dealing with blood of a mere human being; not blood of animals, but the Blood of the Son of the Living God. The Blood of Jesus is central to the Gospel message, because without the shedding of Blood there is no remission or removal of sin.

It is the Blood of Jesus that enables God Almighty in His glory and holiness to be able to look upon a vile sinner and remove his sin. Without the Blood, the Church will fall into the trap of New Age thinking. The Bible says that without the shedding of blood there is no remission (Hebrews 9:22). More particularly in these days when there is a surge in wickedness, evil, and satanic activities, the Church of God needs to bring forth the testimony of the Blood, as it is by means of this Blood we overcome the evil one (Revelation 12:11). Without the Blood, the message of repentance will be lost, as it is the Blood that encourages us to come into a place of humbleness, brokenness, and repentance. The shedding of the Blood of Jesus presupposes that man is a fallen creature and helpless to save himself so the Son of God paid our ransom

The Cross

The Cross as a message and lifestyle is at the heart of the Gospel. If the Church of the Living God does not pay attention and bring back the message of the Cross, we become a generation who will be mostly emotional but cannot take a stand for righteousness. By means of that ugly Cross, God's Best was crucified. By means of that

Cross, we are crucified to the world and the world is crucified to us. The Cross brings us to the place of self-denial. If we do not come to the place of self-denial, we will only have an academic Christianity that cannot be respected by God and which cannot impress the devil. God doesn't mind how much we sing about His love for us (which is real anyway), but He just wants us to be like Him and the Cross forces us to embrace the narrow way in our lives. *"For the preaching of the cross is to them that perish foolishness; but unto us which are saved it is the power of God"* (1Corinthians 1:18). The Church must return to simple messages on the Cross.

Intimacy with God

God not only loves us; God is in love with us. The Lord God wants to be with His people. At one point, He told me that He would allow the Holy Spirit to take the love between Himself and Jesus and transmit it to the Church. When He said that, all the glory of heaven was unleashed upon me; I was melting where I was.

God wants us to hunger and thirst for Him. David cried out, *"O God, thou art my God; early will I seek thee: my soul thirsteth for thee, my flesh longeth for thee in a dry and thirsty land, where no water is"* (Psalm 63:1). We must return to a place of intimacy with our God. It is a privilege for us to love Him, because He first loved us. The message and lifestyle of intimacy with God will open the door to new possibilities in the supernatural realm of Almighty God. We at the church of God must return to the message of intimacy and the pursuit of God. Let us love Him, let us chase after Him. He delights in it.

The Power of the Almighty

When we become intimate with God, we enter into the power side of the Almighty. The gospel is not in mere words. It is also in demonstration of the Spirit and of the power. This generation cannot be saved with philosophy and sound doctrines alone. This generation must be confronted with the raw power of God. That is what God is calling us to to embrace His power. As we get intimate with Him and He begins to adjust us, we will move into the realm of power. The age in which we live has seen an upsurge in counterfeit power in all shapes and forms invading all religions. The devil is anxious to take over, but it is not his time. This is the time that God wants to raise a glorious Church, put His seal of authority on the sons and daughters of the Living God who will be able to give this generation a demonstration of the resurrection power of the Lord Jesus. This is the desire of the Lord. Go for the power of the Holy Spirit. It will take power to break shackles, to bring changes, to transform societies and nations. God said to tell His children to desire power. He warned me in a revelation that the power of the Holy Spirit would be decisive and that those who do not pay the price to walk in His power would live as beggars, because all His provisions would flow from His power to His children.

Evangelism

Power is for purpose. Power without purpose is abuse and ultimate destruction. God wants us to evangelize, to craft ways and means to reach the lost, to spend our time and our money to reach the lost. If the Church of the present day does not rise up to reach out to the lost the consequence will be that we will be hardened in our consciences. We will be practicing self-hypnosis, that is we will be so concerned about our own needs to the point that we will not see what God has done. In the wilderness, God sent the Israelites manna every day. When that day's supply was done, they forgot about it. He had to send it again the next morning, and by the evening they had forgotten again and rebelled. Miracles without focus on the purpose of evangelism will lead to hardness of heart. God wants His Church to return to the purpose for which he came, which is to seek and save that which was lost.

Eternity

Most Christians are living from time to eternity, and that is wrong. God invites us to live in eternity now. Once you are born again, you do not wait to die to enjoy eternity. You are in eternity now. What is the advantage of living from eternity through time? That way, you are judging yourself day to day. People are so blessed today that they enjoy the blessing and forget that heaven is their home. What will it benefit us if we gain the whole world and lose our souls? By living in eternity, we will be able to shun sinful behavior and avoid the traps that Satan puts all over the place by way of temptation. We will be able to live an accountable life, always cognizant that we are pilgrims on the earth, hasting unto the day of the Lord, putting all our energy knowing that heaven is real. Sin will not be able to overtake us.

These are the seven urgent messages the Lord wants the Church to reckon with. If you are reading this, God bless you!

BREAKTHROUGH PROPHETIC DELIVERANCE PRAYERS

THE GREATEST PRAYER OF A LIFETIME

The greatest prayer of a lifetime is to be reconnected back to God in a living relationship. A relationship is a basis for asking. You cannot pray to a God whom you don't know and who does not know you. God wants to be intimate with you. This type of relationship is available to each one of us when we sincerely repent of our sins, ask for God's forgiveness, and receive His Son, Jesus, as our personal Lord and Savior. If you have never surrendered your life to God, or if you have turned away from God and you want to return to Him, now is the time. God is waiting for you. His arms are open wide to receive you. Just pray this simple prayer right now:

O Lord, be merciful to me, a sinner. I realize that I am a sinner. I need a Savior and you are my savior. I repent of every sin, every wrongdoing, and I ask for your forgiveness. I receive Jesus Christ, Your only begotten

Son, as my Lord and my Savior. I believe that Jesus went to the cross for me and paid the price for my salvation, and now I receive Him into my heart. I declare that I am born again. I am a child of God. Old sins are gone, and I have a brand-new life in Christ in Jesus' name. Amen.

APPENDIX

PRACTICAL DELIVERANCE ENCOUNTERS

CASE OF DELAY IN MARRIAGE

S is. W was a 36 year old, anointed believer and she approached me and said, "Pastor Patrick, what is my problem? Here I am at 36 years old. I have been a dedicated follower of Jesus for 19 years and all these years, no man has ever proposed marriage to me so that I have the opportunity to say yes or no. What is wrong with me?" I have had many people say that to me but on this occasion, I knew that Sis. W was very serious and needed answers. I scheduled with her to go on a 3-day fast together, seeking the Lord to find out what was wrong.

On the set day of the fast, I went before the Lord on my knees to present the case and I drifted away in a trance. I saw four huge, ferocious dogs advancing menacingly towards me. Speaking with a human voice, they asked me, "Is it by power? Is it by power?" I responded by saying, "It is not by power nor by might, but by My Spirit says the Lord. I take up the *authority of the name of Jesus and come against you." I opened my eyes. I was shocked and said, "My goodness! Lord, what is this?" He said that these are Abaddon powers in charge of her family. The word Abaddon means Destruction. It is a principality in charge of lawlessness and immorality. This was the power that was in charge of her family and was hindering her from getting married.*

On the third day we met to pray. She was kneeling before me and I was praying in the spirit to the Lord for intervention and deliverance. All of a sudden I got carried away and transported into the future to witness her marriage. The marriage was a powerful, gorgeous marriage and I came back to myself speaking in tongues. I said to her, "Sister, open your eyes. I just attended your wedding." Then I started prophesying: "Sister, you have two months to take the veil from your face or you will miss it." A veil means spiritual blindness of some sorts. Satan uses them to blindside us and abort our seasons. We prayed and ended the session. Of course, in a short time, she disconnected from me. I understand that when she realized that I was a bachelor but was not the one God chose for her, she became angry. (Lord could that have been part of the veil?) I did not know that she was looking towards me. Exactly two months after this, a very important military officer who lived 400 miles away came and proposed marriage to her.

IMPORTANT LESSONS

1. *Here we can see that sometimes people struggle because there are unseen powers, causing delays and are blocking them. It will take deliverance warfare to dismantle such barriers. When knowledge of deliverance is lacking, people just endure painful delays thinking that they are waiting on the Lord.*

2. **Wrong thoughts or Focus:** *Our own thought patterns can sometimes hinder or cause us needless delays. The fasting provided us the opportunity to take care of this. The Lord then warned her to take off a veil that was standing in the way or again miss a marital miracle that was on God's calendar for her within two months. This brings me to a third issue which is missed opportunities and aborted seasons.*

3. *Missed opportunities and aborted seasons. We see from the above that God had scheduled an appointment for her breakthrough and that appointment was just eight weeks away. Had I not taken her into fasting, she could not have known about it and such ignorance will be used by the enemy to their own advantage. How? Remember*

that the Lord said she had to take away the veil! A form of spiritual blindness imposed by the enemy to blindside her and rob her by then aborting her season. Painful delay blows from the evil one are frequently inflicted on God's people who mostly walk in ignorance of their times and seasons thereby failing to prepare for the blessings and opportunities that God programmed into those seasons for their promotions. "My people are destroyed for lack of Knowledge" Hosea 4:6.

A MISLEADING VOICE

Here is a similar case to the one referenced above. We were conducting a deliverance crusade in a particular city in Lagos, Nigeria. The Word of Knowledge came and the man of God said, "There is someone here whose life is going in the wrong direction because you a listening to a misleading voice." Once that word went out, the power of God hit a particular woman. I noticed that some of our pastors were trying very hard to get the demons out of her. This normally infuriates me, and I walked over to them and asked, "Why are you working so hard? Step aside." I said, "In the name of Jesus, I command the manifestations to cease." This is how I was led. I normally listen in my spirit. I commanded that the sister's spirit should take charge over her body. She sobered up and I said to her, "Sister, do you want deliverance?" She said no! I was shocked. I said to the pastors, "this sister said that she does not want deliverance, and this is why you are struggling." I asked her, "Why, then, did you come here?"

She answered, "I didn't come for myself; I came for my friend. Maybe God will answer her. I have been waiting on God for many years pleading with Him. I came out of an Islamic family. Everyone is laughing at me. I was pleading with God, just for His own namesake, to please give me a husband and He would not do it. So I don't care about myself anymore. He is not going to answer me." Oh no! This was not God denying her the blessing but rather a spirit of delay and a misleading voice causing her frustrations. The word of God says that every perfect gift, every good gift comes from heaven. God wants to bless. But when a spirit of delay and a misleading voice combine together, and deliverance is not known, the strategy of the wicked becomes effective.

IMPORTANT LESSONS

To be successful in Deliverance cases we must carefully listen to the Holy Spirit instruction and follow His strategy accurately. Let's do a little analysis of the above scenario. The word of knowledge started off this Deliverance and notice that the Lord said there was the presence and work of a misleading spirit/voice. The power of God's Holy Spirit immediately interacted with the woman in question and the demons were rattled and violent manifestations began as the demons struggled for their very lives under the weight of God's power. The Pastors jumped in and started attempting to get the demons out of her. This was right but they failed because they did not yield grounds to the Holy Spirit for complete discernment but instead relied only on their God given authority of the name of Jesus to cast out the demons. Indeed they had that authority and the demons stood inferior to them yet it appears they were mostly reacting to the manifestation and in this way allowed the devil to gain the upper hand. In all circumstances, we are to reverently yield consciously to the Holy Spirit's instruction even when moving in commanding authority against the devil. We should be reverently responding to the active leading of the Holy Spirit and not excited in the flesh and reacting to the devil's drama. Without the Lord, the Holy Spirit, we can do nothing. Moreover, this individual had swallowed the devil's lie thereby validating his presence; merely using your authority to cast out the demons will not last and they could easily jump back in. She needed some good teaching in the Word of God regarding her wrong notions about God's love for her. I merely interrupted the drama, corrected the Pastors and allowed them to continue while I moved on to other cases. Yes the demons were eventually cast out but first a brief counseling to secure her understanding and brokenness was required to re-engineer things in the correct direction.

OVERCOMING DELAY FACTORS IN DELIVERANCE

BLOOD OF GOD:
A CASE OF DECEPTION

This case involves a very dangerous spirit of deception. It happened many years ago, around 1995 in the city of Ibadan, Nigeria. Some of my financial partners had reached out to a certain unique couple in their own evangelism efforts who wanted to receive deliverance ministry and they thought that I could help. This couple was strange in the sense that the man was a Marine medium. A marine medium is someone who is in touch with Marine spirits and professes some type of false prophetic. Mermaid spirits can manifest divination through python or serpentine spirit and in this way, develop clients people who come for prophetic visions and insights.

This man was some type of demonic Prince, practicing his evil craft and obviously doing good business for himself and his master Satan, until Jesus came calling and he gave his life to Christ. There was a young woman he wanted to marry and both of them had become involved in that trade and by the time they came to me for deliverance, their story began to develop an interesting twist. Quite interestingly, as I counseled them, some bizarre things started happening. Every time they came to me for counseling, the demon spirit they were in touch with told them, "That man is a true man of God. The things he is telling you, you must take seriously. Go through the prayers and get married so that I can enter your womb and you can give birth to me. I want to be born as a human being so that I can escape the judgment of God. Only the blood can save." This spirit claimed to have originated in the Mediterranean. It told them of experiencing Noah's Flood. In their kingdom, according to the spirit, there was pandemonium as they were rattled by the fact that time is very short; the wrath of God will soon begin, and he wanted to be saved before it begins to rain fire and brimstone. The only hope for it (the demon spirit) to be saved was the couple (Medium) to get married and give birth to it (the demon spirit). The whole scenario was very confusing to me for a while. I had never had a demon spirit advocating Scriptures like that. I went before the Father, and told Him that I did not understand, and that I needed Him to clarify my thoughts. I did not want to get into error. Why should this spirit be validating? Where in the Scripture does it say this? As I started to ask the Lord, I was at the point of near confusion.

The Lord came to me mercifully and said, "Ask them if the spirit is saying the blood of God or the Blood of Jesus." When they came for counseling again, I inquired what the Lord told me to ask. When they said the blood of God, I realized that it definitely was a demon spirit who could not say "the Blood of Jesus"

I asked the Lord, how come the demon spirit was confirming His Word and He said that there is a general desperation and this demon was so desperate that even though it knew that a demon spirit cannot be saved, was trying to see if he could get a human body through them and therefore probably be saved. I do not believe that this is possible but it shows a level of desperation in the spirit world.

IMPORTANT LESSONS

As we go deep into deliverance work, we will encounter things that ears cannot even comprehend. People may think that we have gone out of our minds. The couple were eventually set free but the lady was a bit difficult and emotional about the spirit once I concluded it was a demon and needed to be cast out and the door shut against it. The man, the would be husband intervened and called the lady (his spouse) to order in the following words; the beautiful, graceful woman you have come to know and love as the

(Mommy spirit) is not the original image and look of this spirit. The original state is a hideous and fearful looking creature with snake heads. The lady gave in to reason and the demon spirit was evicted.

We will encounter what the Bible calls the depth of satan but let's be clear, the Word of God is settled forever. We are to hold the written Word above experiences and judge everything and everyone on that basis. If we do this, we will not fall into deception and demonic delusion. This is partly why we are to be under authority and be accountable.

Bibliography

Watchman Nee, (January 1980) The Latent Power of the Soul. Christian Fellowship Publishers Inc. , New York

Derek Prince; (1998) They Shall Expel Demons (Your Invisible Enemies) Bakers Publishing Group, Ada Michigan.

John Simpson and Edmund Weiner (Editors) Oxford English Dictionary Online. Oxford University Press Publication. 1989

Eto Victoria, Lesson Notes on Deliverance; (1986) Shalom Christian Mission, Ozoro, Delta State, Nigeria.

Hinn Benny, (2011) Angels and Demons, Bookmark Publishing Dallas, Texas USA

Obode O. Jerome, 90 Keys to Effective Praying AuthorHouse, UK

ABOUT THE AUTHOR

Dr. Patrick Odigie is a man graced with prophetic insights, revelations, and his ministry is marked by signs, wonders, and demonstrations of the Spirit. The Ministry of this Apostolic Prophet, spanning three decades, has taken him to four Continents and he is mandated by God to mobilize the Praying Power of the Church to unleash end-time revival and Healing of the Nations. Patrick Odigie functions under a powerful anointing of Counsel, revelations, dreams interpretations and encounters in the spirit realm.

He is a trained Deliverance minister, substance abuse counselor and a consultant/participant at World Forum of Drug Demand Reduction, Bangkok, Thailand, in December 1994 under the auspices of United Nations Drug Control Program for Non- Governmental

Organizations. Brother Odigie is an alumnus of the prestigious Haggai Institute of Advanced Christian Leadership, Maui, Hawaii.

He presently resides in Uniondale New York where He and his wife, Rev. Mabel Odigie, Oversees the Prophetic Power house Ministries; and travels extensively throughout the Nation mobilizing churches and Christian fellowship groups to unleash the power of the praying church for end-time healing revival. The three cord focus of his message is Prayer, Sacrifice, and Intimacy with the Holy Spirit as pre-requisites for accessing the power of God for the end-time healing revival.

He sees himself as an extreme lover of Jesus, and seeks to promote a spirit of bridal love for the Lord everywhere. Patrick is married to his best friend, Pastor Mabel Odigie, and is blessed with three anointed and prophetic children; Praise, Honor and Favor.

Other Books by
THE AUTHOR

Foundations for True and Complete Deliverance

Warriors Guide on Effective Deliverance Ministry

War is Normal

Deliverance That Works

Destiny Under Fire

The Anointing of The Curse Breaker

Prophetic Gateways